Donald Davie is the foremost literary critic of
his generation and one of its leading poets.
His career has been marked by a series of
challenging and original critical interventions
on American, British and East European
literature, of which this is the latest. The eighteenth century is the great age of the English
hymn, though these powerful and popular
texts have been marginalised in the formation
of the conventional literary canon. These are
poems which have been put to the test of
experience by a wider public than that
generally envisaged by literary criticism, and
have been kept alive by congregations in each
generation. Davie's study of the eighteenth-
century hymn and metrical psalm brings to
light a body of literature forgotten as poetry:
work by Charles Wesley and Christopher
Smart, Isaac Watts and William Cowper,
together with several poets unjustly neglected,
such as the mysterious John Byron. In the
process Davie reveals the nature of eighteenth-
century transformations of biblical texts,
and offers insight into the relationship of
Christopher Smart's literary style to the
aesthetics of English rococo. Davie's new book
reclaims for our attention a rich and humanly
important literary genre. After this it can no
longer be said that the eighteenth century
produced little or no lyric poetry.

s poetry and
erary criti-
fessor of
rsity before his
h Academy,
ships at
ited States
er. Over ten
her with two
ppeared since
es *Purity of*
iculate Energy
und: Poet as
l British Poetry
erature of the
0 (1978) and

Donald Davie is the foremost literary critic of his generation and one of its leading poets. His career has been marked by a series of challenging and original critical interventions on American, British and East European literature, of which this is the latest. The eighteenth century is the great age of the English hymn, though these powerful and popular texts have been marginalized in the formation of the conventional literary canon. These are poems which have been put to the test of experience by a wider public than that generally envisaged by literary criticism, and have been kept alive by congregations in each generation. Davie's study of the eighteenth-century hymn and metrical psalm brings to light a body of literature forgotten as poetry: work by Charles Wesley and Christopher Smart, Isaac Watts and William Cowper, together with several poets unjustly neglected, such as the mysterious John Byrom. In the process Davie reveals the nature of eighteenth-century transformations of biblical texts, and offers insight into the relationship of Christopher Smart's literary style to the aesthetics of the English rococo. Davie's new book reclaims for our attention a rich and humanly important literary genre. After this it can no longer be said that the eighteenth century produced little or no lyric poetry.

CAMBRIDGE STUDIES IN EIGHTEENTH-CENTURY
ENGLISH LITERATURE AND THOUGHT   19

The Eighteenth-Century Hymn in England

CAMBRIDGE STUDIES IN EIGHTEENTH-CENTURY ENGLISH LITERATURE AND THOUGHT

General Editors
Dr HOWARD ERSKINE-HILL, Litt.D., FBA,
Pembroke College, Cambridge
and Professor JOHN RICHETTI,
University of Pennsylvania

Editorial Board
Morris Brownell, *University of Nevada*
Leopold Damrosch, *Harvard University*
J. Paul Hunter, *University of Chicago*
Isobel Grundy, *University of Alberta*
Lawrence Lipking, *Northwestern University*
Harold Love, *Monash University*
Claude Rawson, *Yale University*
Pat Rogers, *University of South Florida*
James Sambrook, *University of Southampton*

This series is designed to accommodate monographs and critical studies on authors, works, genres and other aspects of literary culture from the later part of the seventeenth century to the end of the eighteenth. Since academic engagement with this field has become an increasingly interdisciplinary enterprise, books will be especially encouraged which in some way stress the cultural context of the literature, or examine it in relation to contemporary art, music, philosophy, historiography, religion, politics, social affairs and so on.

Recent titles in this series include

Eighteenth-Century Sensibility and the Novel: The Senses in Social Context
by Ann Jessie Van Sant

Family and the Law in Eighteenth-Century Fiction: The Public Conscience in the Private Sphere
by John P. Zomchick

Crime and Defoe: A New Kind of Writing
by Lincoln B. Faller

Literary Transmission and Authority: Dryden and Other Writers
edited by Earl Miner and Jennifer Brady

Plots and Counterplots: Sexual Politics and the Body Politic in English Literature, 1660–1730
by Richard Braverman

A complete list of books in the series is given at the end of the volume

Rook Lane Congregational Church, Frome.

The Eighteenth-Century
Hymn in England

DONALD DAVIE

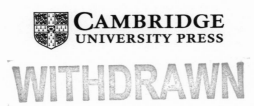

CAMBRIDGE
UNIVERSITY PRESS

Published by the Press Syndicate of the University of Cambridge
The Pitt Building, Trumpington Street, Cambridge CB2 1RP
40 West 20th Street, New York, NY 10011–4211, USA
10 Stamford Road, Oakleigh, Victoria 31656, Australia

First published 1993

Printed in Great Britain at the University Press, Cambridge

A catalogue record for this book is available from the British Library

Library of Congress cataloguing in publication data
Davie, Donald.
The eighteenth-century hymn in England / by Donald Davie.
p.   cm. – (Cambridge studies in eighteenth-century English
literature and thought)
Includes index.
ISBN 0 521 38168 1
1. Hymns, English – History and criticism.
2. English poetry – 18th century – History and criticism.
I. Title.   II. Title: 18th-century hymn in England.   III Series
BV312.D33   1993
264′.2′094209033–dc20   92–46204   CIP

ISBN 0 521 38168 1 hardback

Contents

Illustrations

Introduction

In Rudyard Kipling's story, 'At the End of the Passage' (from *Life's Handicap*, 1891), four young Englishmen foregather somewhere in the plains of India during an outbreak of cholera. Bored by cards and other ways of passing the time, one of them called Mottram manages to coax some melodies from the host's dilapidated piano. After picking out some music-hall tunes, a dust-storm having meanwhile passed over the house, he modulates to something else:

In the silence after the storm he glided from the more directly personal songs of Scotland, half humming them as he played, into the Evening Hymn.

'Sunday,' said he, nodding his head.

'Go on. Don't apologise for it,' said Spurstow.

Hummil laughed long and riotously. 'Play it, by all means. You're full of surprises today. I didn't know you had such a gift of finished sarcasm. How does that thing go?'

Mottram took up the tune.

'Too slow by half. You miss the note of gratitude,' said Hummil. 'It ought to go to the "Grasshopper's Polka" – this way.' And he chanted, *prestissimo* –

> 'Glory to thee, my God, this night,
> For all the blessings of the light.

That shows we really feel our blessings. How does it go on? –

> If in the night, I sleepless lie,
> My soul with secret thoughts supply;
> May no ill dreams disturb my rest –

Quicker, Mottram! –

> Or powers of darkness me molest!'

'Bah! what an old hypocrite you are!'

It has often been remarked how constantly Kipling, who was only by the loosest definition a Christian writer, alludes to the Authorized Version of the Scriptures and sometimes to the Book of Common

1

Prayer. This passage shows that he took for granted in himself and in his readers no less familiarity with the body of English hymnody. It is notable that the author of the Evening Hymn is not so much as named. And this must mean either that Kipling could take it for granted that all his readers would know the author, or else (more probably and more intriguingly) that Kipling and his readers thought the hymn virtually anonymous, so thoroughly had it been taken over into the common stock, quite as if it were a folk-song or a ballad. We seem required to suppose that by 1891 certain English hymns had entered into the national consciousness so far as to furnish allusions and commonplaces even for those not religiously disposed.

However, if this justifies us in giving to congregational hymns more attention than is normally given to them in accounts of our literary heritage, at the same time it shows how much resistance there will be to any such enterprise. Because certain hymns have become so thoroughly incorporated into a notion of English nationhood, English people will be affronted by any attempt to consider them judiciously, as poems. Kipling's story gives us all the evidence:

> 'Don't be an ass,' said Lowndes. 'You are at full liberty to make fun of anything else, but leave that hymn alone. It's associated in my mind with the most sacred recollections...'
>
> 'Summer evenings in the country ... stained-glass window ... light going out, and you and she jamming your heads together over one hymn-book,' said Mottram.
>
> 'Yes, and a fat old cockchafer hitting you in the eye when you walked home. Smell of hay, and a moon as big as a bandbox sitting on the top of a haycock; bats ... roses ... milk and midges,' said Lowndes.
>
> 'Also mothers. I can just recollect my mother singing me to sleep with that when I was a little chap,' said Spurstow.

This is mawkish and embarrassing, and hard to credit as the work of one who would go on to be a great writer in both verse and prose. Yet the testimony cannot be disregarded; such are the tender feelings, not specifically religious, which even today may be bruised by a plain declaration that the Evening Hymn, like Thomas Ken's other hymns, is very indifferent writing:

> All praise to Thee, my god, this night,
> For all the blessings of the light.
> Keep me, O keep me, King of kings,
> Beneath Thy own almighty wings.

Forgive me, Lord, for Thy dear Son,
The ill that I this day have done;
That with the world, myself, and Thee,
I ere I sleep at peace may be.

Teach me to live, that I may dread
The grave as little as my bed;
To die, that this vile body may
Rise glorious at the awful day.

O may my soul on Thee repose,
And may sweet sleep mine eyelids close;
Sleep that may me more vig'rous make,
To serve my God when I awake.

When in the night I sleepless lie,
My soul with heavenly thoughts supply;
Let no ill dreams disturb my rest,
No power of darkness me molest.

Dull sleep, of sense me to deprive,
I am but half my time alive;
Thy faithful lovers, Lord, are griev'd
To lie so long of Thee bereav'd.

But tho' sleep o'er my frailty reigns,
Let it not hold me long in chains:
And now and then let loose my heart,
Till it an hallelujah dart.

The faster sleep the senses binds,
The more unfetter'd are our minds;
O may my soul, from matter free,
Thy loveliness unclouded see!

O when shall I in endless day
For ever chase dark sleep away,
And hymns with the supernal choir
Incessant sing and never tire!

O may my Guardian while I sleep,
Close to my bed his vigils keep,
His love angelical instil,
Stop all the avenues of ill.

May he celestial joy rehearse,
And thought to thought with me converse
Or in my stead, all the night long,
Sing to my God a grateful song.

> Praise God from whom all blessings flow,
> Praise Him, all creatures here below,
> Praise Him above, ye heavenly host,
> Praise Father, Son, and Holy Ghost.

Of these twelve stanzas not more than six or at most seven have ever normally been sung. And this speaks for itself: a good poem is an organism too delicate to be subjected to, and survive, such drastic amputation. Ken's companion-piece, his 'Morning Hymn', is an equivalent case. But to say so may still give offence, though certainly to fewer people now than a hundred years ago. The offence will be aggravated for those, more religiously inclined, who recognize in Bishop Ken a *saint*. His saintliness has never been denied, even by those who would find it hard to tease out the very delicate issues of conscience which preoccupied him and his fellow non-jurors as they tried to balance, in the decades after James II had been forced from the throne, the claims upon them of the State and the Church. In fact it is a pity that Ken, the ejected Bishop of Bath and Wells, has enjoyed such pre-eminence among the non-jurors. One needs Canon Overton's book of 1902[1] to be reminded how many non-jurors there were; how not just six fellow-bishops, but hundreds of more obscure people, both clerical and lay, were prepared to forego worldly advancement and prosperity for the sake of a principle. It brings home what is too seldom said: that England under William and Mary and Queen Anne, and for some time after, was a devoutly Christian society. Those who admire Ken and his fellows for integrity in politics as well as for piety and learning may well think that pointing to Ken's deficiencies as a poet is, while doubtless legitimate, trivial.

A similar case is that of the nonconformist Philip Doddridge (1702–51), who appears to have been not much if at all less saintly than Thomas Ken.[2] And possibly Kipling's four men in India who remembered Ken's Evening Hymn would have recognized some hymns by Doddridge, no less well loved:

> Oh God of Bethel, by whose Hand
> Thine Israel still is fed
> Who thro' this weary Pilgrimage
> Hast all our Fathers led,

[1] J. H. Overton, *The Nonjurors. Their Lives, Principles, and Writings* (1902).
[2] See Malcolm Deacon, *Philip Doddridge of Northampton* (Northampton, 1980).

To thee our humble Vows we raise
　　To thee address our Prayer
And in thy kind and faithful Breast
　　Deposite all our Care.

If thou thro' each perplexing Path
　　Wilt be our constant Guide,
If thou wilt daily Bread supply
　　And Raiment wilt provide,

If thou wilt spread thy Shield around
　　Till these our wandrings cease
And at our Father's lov'd Abode
　　Our Souls arrive in Peace,

To thee as to our Covenant God
　　We'll our whole selves resign
And count that not our tenth alone
　　But all we have is thine.

H. Leigh Bennett, writing in John Julian's *Dictionary of Hymnology* (1892), certainly spoke for a consensus when he thought that Doddridge as a hymn-writer could be named in the same breath with his mentor and forerunner Isaac Watts. Doddridge's hymns, Bennett decided, 'have not the power or the richness of Watts, and a deficiency of ear gives them thinness of tone'. But, he goes on, 'they excel Watts in simplicity, serenity, and tenderness'. And he goes so far as to deny that any hymn by Watts is 'so perfect in the combined qualities of feeling, structure, melody, and diction' as Doddridge's 'My god, and is Thy table spread'. But however it may be with that Communion hymn, it is surely clear that only in the last two lines of 'Oh God of Bethel' does Doddridge achieve Watts' *strength*, in the sense that the seventeenth and eighteenth centuries gave to that term, meaning resonant conciseness. Bennett's 'power' and 'richness' are by contrast windy words, with no readily assignable meanings. And as for 'simplicity, serenity, and tenderness', one may suspect these are tributes to the saintliness of the author rather than to any qualities in his verses. But for persons of a certain estimable kind – still to be found, though less numerous than in 1891 – such a hymn has a devotional significance, and cherished associations, which they will think impugned and side-tracked by the cool judgement that as a poem it is competent and fluent, but not much more. No more can be said for the most prominent woman hymnist of the century, the Baptist Anne Steele (1716–78).

Doddridge was not named by John Keble in his essay, 'Sacred Poetry'.[3] Indeed no eighteenth-century hymn-writer is there named, except for Cowper, who is made to suffer by comparison with Burns, in a tendentiously rigged competition between two passages of verse which have, in the matter of genre, nothing in common. Ken, however, figures quite largely; and yet Keble's remarks on him, though plainly meant to be laudatory, are to say the least ambivalent:

After Milton, sacred poetry seems to have greatly declined, both in the number and merit of those who cultivated it. No other could be expected from the conflicting evils of those times: in which one party was used to brand every-thing sacred with the name of Puritanism, and the other to suspect everything poetical of being contrary to morality and religion.

Yet most of the great names of that age, especially among the Romanists, as Dryden, Pope, and before them Habington, continued to dedicate some of their poetry to religion. By their faith they were remote from the controversies which agitated the established Church, and their devotion might indulge itself without incurring the suspicion of a fanatical spirit. Then the solemnity of their worship is fitted to inspire splendid and gorgeous strains, such as Dryden's paraphrase of the 'Veni Creator'; and their own fallen fortunes in England, no less naturally, would fill them with a sense of decay very favourable to the plaintive tenderness of Habington and Crashaw.

A feeling of this kind, joined to the effect of distressing languor and sickness, may be discerned, occasionally, in the writings of Bishop Ken; though he was far indeed from being a Romanist. We shall hardly find, in all ecclesiastical history, a greener spot than the later years of this courageous and affectionate pastor; persecuted alternately by both parties, and driven from his station in his declining age; yet singing on, with unabated cheerfulness, to the last. His poems are not popular, nor, probably, ever will be ... [Keble was wrong here, as we have seen]; but whoever in earnest loves his three well-known hymns, and knows how to value such unaffected strains of poetical devotion, will find his account, in turning over his four volumes, half narrative and half lyric, and all avowedly on sacred subjects; the narrative often cumbrous and the lyric verse not seldom languid and redundant: yet all breathing such an angelic spirit, interspersed with such pure and bright touches of poetry, that such a reader as we have supposed will scarcely find it in his heart to criticise them.

The tenderness towards Rome of the Tractarian Keble is much in evidence. (William Habington for instance (1605–64) was a Roman Catholic who included sacred poems in the 1640 edition of his *Castara*, originally 1634.) But it is not sectarian bias that stops Keble doing justice to his eighteenth-century forerunners. His theory of poetry

---

[3] *Quarterly Review*, 1825. In John Keble, *Occasional Papers and Reviews* (Oxford, 1877).

would have excluded them anyway, as was apparent from the lectures he gave (in Latin) as Professor of Poetry at Oxford. Keble cannot be ignored, because in the long run he was influential and also, it is fair to say, because his practice as a poet was so much better than his theory. That theory was much more restrictive and extreme than Wordsworth's, which Keble seems to have thought he was taking over and extending, and more categorical than that of Matthew Arnold who, as Keble's successor in the Oxford professorship, nevertheless took over from his predecessor enough of his prejudices to ensure that eighteenth-century poetry would not get a fair hearing in the rest of the nineteenth century nor indeed through much of the twentieth. Particularly pernicious was, as we see from Keble's remarks on Ken, his judging poetry on the moral and spiritual merits of the poets, rather than on the artistic merits or demerits of their compositions. This slide or shuffle is what we see in H. Leigh Bennett's remarks on Doddridge, and indeed it is far from being eliminated from criticism of poetry at the present day.

Wordsworth, it should be noted, was not at all so loftily dismissive of eighteenth-century precedents; Sara Coleridge records that, although Wordsworth heartily applauded Keble's intentions and sentiments in *The Christian Year* (1827), he none the less declared that 'there is better poetry in Watts than in Keble'.[4] And surely we can only follow Wordsworth's example. Purity of intention in the poet, sweetness of disposition, saintliness of behaviour – these may be, and should be, extolled in the right place. But they can carry no weight, or very little, in the examination of those poets' poetry.

Still further off the mark is any consideration of our poets' behaviour and sentiments in public affairs. It so happens that all the poets who wrote the best hymns appear to have been, as modern opinion regards the matter, Tories. This is true even of Isaac Watts who, as a Cromwellian Independent, might have been expected to harbour republican sympathies. There is no evidence that he did so; on the contrary, to any one who like Watts took seriously the scriptural witness of David, King and Psalmist, a devout monarchism was hardly to be avoided. For anti-monarchical, egalitarian and 'radical' sentiments in well-composed hymns, we have to wait till the next century: for Ebenezer Elliott or (more dubiously) James Montgomery. This is what an impartial survey of the evidence enforces. To those for whom the socio-political bearings of poetry are the most interesting thing about it, this will be

---

[4] See Brian W. Martin, *John Keble: Priest, Professor and Poet* (1976), p. 74.

unwelcome news. But all the poets we are to consider were concerned primarily with the vertical relationship of man with God, only secondarily with the horizontal relationships of man with his fellows. Since this was their main concern, it seems only fair to consider their writings from the same point of view. Neither Ken nor Doddridge would fare better from another standpoint.

What must in any case be rejected is the very common and assiduously promoted notion that England in 1700 or 1740 was an irreligious nation. Ken's life and Doddridge's (with others, for instance William Law's) are thus relevant to this study, though their writings are not. Sanctity was possible in early Hanoverian England; it was aimed at, and sometimes attained – doubtless by obscure persons, as well as by those we can name. Unless that is acknowledged, the great hymns which are a glory of that period will seem to float unanchored, in a sort of historical limbo.

Sanctity is a high destiny to which few are called. To establish a fitting context for the eighteenth-century congregational hymn, it is necessary to remember less the necessarily few saints than the much more numerous worried and scrupulous worshippers, though of these we know inevitably only those who had a relatively high rank in society. One such was William, fifth Baron Digby (1662–1752), the non-juror honoured by the Roman Catholic Alexander Pope. Digby's decent and modest life has been painstakingly and affectingly unearthed by Howard Erskine-Hill.[5] Digby, Erskine-Hill persuades us, was representative, a fervent churchman 'whose outlook and deeds were moulded in that remarkably earnest and evangelical phase of Anglicanism, at the end of the seventeenth century and beginning of the eighteenth, which fostered the rise of the charity schools', and also General Oglethorpe's philanthropic foundation of what became the State of Georgia. 'Earnest' and 'evangelical' are still epithets seldom applied to eighteenth-century England before the emergence of the Wesleys. In later decades one may look to two of Doddridge's converts, both of them reformed rakes. One is Sir James Stonhouse (1716–95), baronet, physician and rector, whose correspondence with his one-time curate Thomas Stedman and with the dissenting patriarch Job Orton, Doddridge's lieutenant and executor, breathes on oecumenical fragrance seldom associated with the England of Wilkes and Pitt, Warbur-

---

[5] Howard Erskine-Hill, *The Social Milieu of Alexander Pope* (New Haven and London, 1975), pp. 132–65, 291.

ton and Bute.[6] A more celebrated case is James Gardiner, killed at Prestonpans in September 1745, whom Doddridge commemorated in *Some Remarkable Passages in the Life of the Honourable Colonel James Gardiner* (1747), a book which Walter Scott acknowledged as his source when he introduced Colonel Gardiner into *Waverley*. Both Stonhouse and Gardiner were obviously exceptional men, but not exceptions to prove the false rule that the English eighteenth century was for the most part sceptical and irreligious. Such people are those we need to bear in mind if we are to attend to the eighteenth-century congregational hymn in England with the seriousness that it deserves.

Doddridge, when he printed in his memoir of Gardiner a hymn of his own which he said was one of Gardiner's favourites, apologizes for it as 'plain'. But a not specially austere taste may think that its plainness elevates it above most of Doddridge's compositions:

> Jesus! I love thy charming Name,
>   'Tis Musick to my Ear:
> Fain would I sound it out so loud,
>   That Earth and Heavn's should hear.
>
> Yes, Thou are precious to my Soul,
>   My Transport and my Trust:
> Jewels to Thee are gaudy Toys,
>   And Gold is sordid Dust.
>
> All my capacious Pow'rs can wish
>   In Thee most richly meet:
> Nor to my Eyes is Life so dear,
>   Nor Friendship half so sweet.
>
> Thy Grace still dwells upon my Heart,
>   And sheds its Fragrance there;
> The noblest Balm of all its Wounds,
>   The Cordial of its Care.
>
> I'll speak the Honours of thy Name
>   With my last lab'ring Breath;
> Then speechless clasp thee in my Arms,
>   The Antidote of Death.

The union of 'all my capacious Pow'rs' with 'the Antidote of Death' is no mean achievement of poetic diction, though it will almost certainly be eliminated from any version of this hymn that we are called on to

---

[6] *Letters from the Rev. Sir J. Stonhouse, Bart., M.D., to the Rev. Thomas Stedman, M.A.* (Shrewsbury, 1800).

sing in public worship. Poetic *diction* indeed may be thought, by earnestly pious people as well as by others with less excuse, a trivial or frivolous concern. However, it is what this study will be principally concerned with.

1

Dr Byrom of Manchester, FRS

John Byrom (1692–1763) is remembered – notably in a plaque on the outside of St Anne's Church, Manchester – as the author of 'Christians, awake! Salute the blessed morn'. In more restricted circles he is known also for the jaunty epigram:

> God bless the King, I mean the Faith's Defender;
> God bless – no Harm in blessing – the Pretender;
> But who Pretender is, or who is King,
> God bless us all – that's quite another Thing.

For Byrom was a Jacobite, or at least did not mind being thought so, making common cause in that with his spiritual mentor, the conspicuous non-juror William Law, who for that scruple forfeited his Cambridge fellowship. Despite the 1715 and 1745 risings, Jacobitism, it appears, for much of Byrom's lifetime was something one could be jaunty about – doubtless because at that time it was hard to say where non-juring ended and Jacobitism began. Maynard Mack[1] calls Byrom 'a poet of sorts'; and if we look at the eight of his poems in David Nichol Smith's *Oxford Book of Eighteenth Century Verse* (1926), we shall think Byrom either a poet of all sorts or else of a very jaunty sort. His poems there are the elegant 'A Pastoral' (from *The Spectator* for 6 October 1714); two epigrams, one of which we have seen; then 'Extempore Verses Upon a Trial of Skill between the Two Great Masters of the Noble Science of Defence, Messrs. Figg and Sutton' (which, says Leslie Stephen, was 'done into prose in Thackeray's *Virginians*'); a poem in twelve six-line stanzas beginning, 'I am Content, I do not care, / Wag as it will the World for me'; then 'Contentment, or The Happy Workman's Song' ('I am a poor Workman as rich as a Jew / A strange sort of Tale, but however 'tis true'); finally, 'Christians, awake!' and a little hymn of no account, 'My spirit longeth for thee'. The uninstructed

---

[1] *Alexander Pope. A Life* (New Haven, 1985), p. 862.

enthusiast reading these pages, so sprightly and genial, colloquial, metrically various and enterprising, may think he has lit on treasure-trove. But he or she has to be disabused; for Leslie Stephen was spiteful but not very wide of the mark when he detected in Byrom 'an almost morbid faculty of rhyming' – he is prolific and facile, and in bulk wearisome.[2]

All the same, we ignore John Byrom at our peril. For the range of interests in this group of poems is reflected in the four volumes of his *Remains* published by the Chetham Society between 1854 and 1857. If we have thought that in Byrom's time an interest in prize-fighting could not go along with an interest in the Gospel, and that the latter could be found only in conventicles and a few deaneries, there is no way to explain John Byrom at all. However it may have been in the metropolis, for Byrom the Mancunian (he was born to ancient landed stock in Lancashire) these interests could be happily indulged side by side, along with amorous and political pleasantries; and as much seems to have been true of some of his numerous correspondents. Stephen says that Byrom's *Remains* 'are among the most interesting illustrations of the social characteristics of his day'. So they are; but the admission comes oddly from one who is more responsible than most for conveying the impression that religious life in the first half of the eighteenth century was characterized by langour and apathy under a dry top-dressing of arguments for and against Deism. Byrom had perhaps an exceptionally sunny disposition; but we cannot think him quite alone in managing to combine quite intense Christian devotion with a hearty appetite for innocent worldly pleasures.

Our eager enthusiast's bewilderment would be aggravated if he chanced to look into another out-of-date anthology, *The Oxford Book of English Mystical Verse* (by D. H. S. Nicholson and A. H. E. Lee, 1917, 1932). Here Byrom is represented by 'A Poetical Version of a Letter from Jacob Behmen', which includes some thoroughly respectable verses:

> For, if the Life of Christ within arise,
> Self-Lust and false Imagination dies, –
> Wholly, it cannot in this present Life,
> But by the Flesh maintains the daily Strife, –
> Dies, and yet lives; as they alone can tell
> In whom Christ fights against the Pow'rs of Hell...

[2] John Byrom, *Poems*, 2 vols. (1773); *Miscellaneous Poems*, 2 vols. (1814).

> These in the Astral Spirit make a Fort,
> Which all the Sins concentre to support;
> And human Will, esteeming for its Joy
> What Christ, to save it, combats to destroy,
> Will not resign the Pride-erected Tow'r,
> Nor live obedient to the Saviour's Pow'r...

No more in literary history than (we may suspect) in church history does the word 'mystical' have a meaning certain enough to carry much weight. But it is safe to suppose that the anthologists did not mean to enrol among mystics Byrom, the connoisseur of pugilists. What qualifies as 'mystical' is the document by Boehme which he versifies; and as to Boehme we need not presume to judge, though we can detect that the picture the poem gives of Christian life is not at all points orthodox. However, the link between Boehme and Byrom was William Law. And Law is a momentous figure, not just for Byrom (and later for the Wesleys, Samuel Johnson and John Keble), but for anyone who wants to assess the spirituality of Hanoverian England.

'Mystic' and 'mystical' figure largely in most modern accounts of Law. His later writings have been edited with a wealth of curious learning by Stephen Hobhouse as *Selected Mystical Writings of William Law* (1938, revised and amplified 1948); and Henri Talon, building on Hobhouse, writes confidently of a 'mystical phase' that Law moved into about 1737.[3] Leslie Stephen, however, whose essay on Law[4] is still valuable, would have no truck with mysticism and, detecting the same change of direction in Law's thinking in the 1730s, defined it differently: 'Religion, then, with Law becomes subjective and emotional, when to almost all his contemporaries it was historical and rational.' If this indeed, a surrender to the irrational, is what happened in mid-career to Law, in his youth a close and caustic polemicist (against Hoadly, Mandeville and Tindal), it was a surrender indeed – though of course what to some minds seems a surrender of reason can to others seem a transcendence of it. Law was a saintly man – this no one has denied, not even those to whom 'saintly' means unworldly, therefore foolish; and the England of George the First was not so rich in saints that what happened to William Law can, for the serious student, be a matter of indifference.

---

[3] Henri Talon's neglected monograph of 1948, *William Law. A Study in Literary Craftsmanship*, has the great merit of comparing Law with his French contemporaries and near-contemporaries.

[4] Leslie Stephen, *Hours in a Library*, 2nd series.

The student of literature will come to suspect that what we have here is a somewhat rudimentary confusion of categories. There is theological writing and there is devotional writing. They overlap in fact and in practice, but in principle they are quite distinct. To a devotional writer like Law, author of *A Serious Call to a Devout and Holy Life* (1728), religion is and has to be, in the end, 'subjective' – in the sense that the doctrines expounded and refined (quite properly) by theologians must in the end be experienced. Better, they must be *tested* by experience. This was what was meant by Law's near-contemporaries, Philip Doddridge and (in America) Isaac Backus, when, to the religion called by modern commentators 'mystical', they attached the term 'experimental'. Having read the theologians, now put their theological conclusions to the proof! Does what they have argued for in fact 'work out', in your experience of private or public devotions? The dogged empiricism of 'experimental' was precisely and consciously what Doddridge and Backus intended. This is not in the least to oppose theology, supposedly 'sterile', to devotion, supposedly warm and emotional; still less to oppose intuition to common sense.[5] We do not act irrationally; on the contrary we follow the dictates of Reason, when, having followed an argument about abstractions, we try to relive (or, more accurately, to *live*) those abstractions in concrete experience. Thus, Law's youthful disputations with theologians were not something from which he weaned himself; on the contrary they were part and parcel of the life of devotion he tried to live himself, and to commend to others.

The capital significance of this for us is that the great congregational hymns of the eighteenth century are certainly devotional writings; they appeal to experience, an experience which they sometimes try to provoke or to ease an entrance for. And yet their peculiar glory is that at their best they are doctrinally exact, scrupulous and specific. Theological niceties are *not* sterile – not so long as they can be translated into worshipping experience. When that happens, their logical niceties can be translated into experiential niceties and, when verbal expression is in question, into linguistic niceties also. There was nothing untoward or incongruous about the so-called Age of Reason having produced the classics of English hymnody; it was just what it should have done – and did.

Byrom, when he wrote religious or 'sacred' poetry, was a theological, not a devotional writer. And that is why the one hymn that we credit him with is not in fact his composition. What he wrote as 'A Hymn for

[5] Leslie Stephen, *Hours in a Library*, 2nd series: 'A sovereign faculty of intuition sets aside the common sense ... '

Christmas Day' is forty-eight lines long, not divided into stanzas. It can
be found in that form in Nichol Smith's *Oxford Book of Eighteenth Century
Verse* and in *The New Oxford Book of Christian Verse*. But what we sing, on
or about Christmas Day, is something else, in six-line stanzas:

> Christians, awake, salute the happy morn
> Whereon the Saviour of mankind was born;
> Rise to adore the mystery of love,
> Which hosts of Angels chanted from above;
> With them the joyful tidings first begun
> Of God Incarnate and the Virgin's Son.
>
> Then to the watchful shepherds it was told,
> Who heard the Angelic herald's voice: 'Behold,
> I bring good tidings of a Saviour's birth
> To you and all the nations upon earth:
> This day hath God fulfilled His promised word.
> This day is born a Saviour, Christ the Lord.'
>
> He spake; and straightway the celestial choir
> In hymns of joy, unknown before, conspire:
> The praises of redeeming love they sang,
> And heaven's whole orb with Alleluias rang;
> God's highest glory was their anthem still,
> Peace upon earth, and unto men good will.
>
> To Bethlehem straight the enlightened shepherds ran,
> To see the wonder God had wrought for man:
> And found, with Joseph and the Blessed Maid,
> Her Son, the Saviour, in a manger laid;
> Then to their flocks, still praising God, return,
> And their glad hearts with holy rapture burn.
>
> Oh! may we keep and ponder in our mind
> God's wondrous love in saving lost mankind;
> Trace we the Babe, Who hath retrieved our loss,
> From His poor manger to His bitter Cross;
> Tread in His steps, assisted by His grace,
> Till man's first heavenly state again takes place.
>
> Then may we hope, the Angelic hosts among,
> To sing, redeemed, a glad triumphal song;
> He that was born upon this joyful day
> Around us all His glory shall display;
> Saved by His love, incessant we shall sing
> Eternal praise to Heaven's Almighty King.

This redaction is the work, it seems, of James Montgomery (1771–1854).[6] Montgomery, raised a Moravian, later a politically radical journalist in Sheffield, is himself an underrated practitioner of sacred poetry. ('Angels, from the realms of glory' is his.) So he is a sober and resourceful workman who preserves some of Byrom's felicities, for instance the way in which 'Rise' at the start of line three means 'Get out of bed', but also something like 'Screw yourselves up'. He eliminates all but one of several references to the Blessed Virgin, presumably to ward off any allegations of Mariolatry. He also eliminates one fine couplet about the shepherds:

> Amazed, the wondrous story they proclaim,
> The first apostles of his infant fame

where the second line is very witty. More to the point is his alteration of the last couplet, which originally read:

> Saved by his love, incessant we shall sing
> Of angels, and of angel-men, the King.

What Montgomery substituted for this, in *The Christian Psalmist* (1825), is what we sing today; and it is certainly less arresting and memorable than what Byrom had written. Yet Montgomery was right to make the change, for it is in the striking expression 'angel-men' that Byrom reveals his allegiance to Boehme; and Montgomery, faithful to his brief to change theological into devotional poetry, rightly eliminates what could impede the devotions of all but those very few (mostly Quakers in fact) who were Behmenist.

This is an important matter, because it compels us towards definitions. What Montgomery has done is to transform a hymn into a *congregational* hymn. For the hymn as a poetic genre is very ancient indeed: the word is derived from the Greek, and certain Greek poems thus styled are so ancient that they have been ascribed to Homer. Indeed, to the ancient Greeks the hymn was something very special. In Book 10 of the *Republic* Socrates is willing to admit only two genres of poetry into the state: 'hymns to the gods and encomia to good men' (607A). And Aristotle in *Poetics* 4 concurs. When Edmund Spenser wrote his Fowre Hymnes ('In Honour of Love', 'In Honour of Beautie', 'of Heavenly Love', 'of Heavenly Beautie'), he was appealing to that

---

[6] See John Julian, *A Dictionary of Hymnology* (1892), p. 231. Julian's work is a monument of late-Victorian scholarship, to set beside Sir James Murray's *Oxford English Dictionary* and *The Dictionary of National Biography*.

ancient Greek precedent, as was James Thomson when in Byrom's lifetime he published 'Hymn on Solitude' (1729), as the atheist Shelley was to do when he wrote 'Hymn to Intellectual Beauty' (1816). It was St Augustine who had tried, unsuccessfully it appears, to harness this illustrious pagan genre to specifically Christian use:

A hymn is the praise of God by singing. A hymn is a song embodying the praise of God. If there be merely praise but not praise of God it is not a hymn. If there be praise, and praise of God, but not sung, it is not a hymn. For it to be a hymn, it is needful, therefore, for it to have three things – praise, praise of God, and these sung.

Augustine's definition seems sufficiently restrictive. But Percy Scholes, who took over Augustine's definition, decided it was not restrictive enough: 'For it to be a hymn it is needful for it to have *four* things – praise, and praise of God, and these sung, and sung by a congregation of people.'[7] Scholes' additional restriction underwrites Montgomery's working assumption that between a hymn and a congregational hymn there are differences, and momentous ones. One of the differences, we notice, is that to be successful a congregational hymn has to be non-sectarian; it must speak to the condition of *all* believers, not to the adherents of any one persuasion, of some one or some few sects.

What we have to do with, then, in the congregational hymns of the eighteenth century, is a body of poems hedged about with restrictions such as – so we are invited to think by current and long-established opinion – no 'true' poet could or should tolerate. If we reflect that the congregations the poet could have in mind varied greatly across space and across time, obeying demographic and socio-economic compulsions that he had no control over, there comes into view another vast range of restrictions that he has to allow for. Plainly therefore this is a body of poetry that challenges at nearly every point those influential theories of poetry which take off from the assumption that the poet has no responsibility except to his own sensibility, his own 'vision'. And so it is easy to see why these writings are commonly excluded from the category of poetry, or are included there only on sufferance, as so many marginal or delimiting cases.

Percy Scholes points out that, whereas Latin hymnody from St Ambrose onwards figures in translation in our hymn-books far more than most of us recognize, yet the original precedents for our congregational hymns are Hebrew: the Psalms of David. Though in the

[7] Percy A. Scholes, *The Oxford Companion to Music* (10th edn, 1970), p. 497.

seventeenth century there was an acrimonious setting up of psalmody against hymnody (turning on the question, how far the words of Holy Scripture could be departed from), for our purposes the distinction is distracting – if only because many of what we sing as hymns are in fact adaptations and paraphrases of psalms. Throughout a century that we still too laxly think of as 'neo-classical', the congregational hymns are there to show that the Hebrew presence was at least as potent as the Graeco-Latin – for the unlettered certainly, but also for sophisticated characters like John Byrom.

Montgomery's redaction of 'Christians, awake!' brings out another feature of the congregational hymn up to and including the eighteenth century, which presents the student with difficulties not encountered with other poems of the period. The hymn-writer did not have copyright in his work as other authors did; and so plagiarism is a concept that does not apply. Because the text of a hymn could be, and was, continually tampered with, we have to deal with these texts as the scholar has learned to deal with texts from folk-literature, like Child's Border Ballads, of which we do not suppose that a late version recorded in perhaps the Ozarks or the Appalachians is an inferior because corrupt version of some pristine original which alone, if we can recover it, deserves our scholarly attention. It would be absurd, and would mistake the whole nature of the genre, to regard Montgomery's version of 'Christians, awake!' as a corruption of Byrom's 'Hymn for Christmas Day'. Apart from anything else, it is the 'corruption' that is part of the experience of worshippers, and lapsed or infrequent worshippers, throughout the English-speaking world. It is easy to be misunderstood about this, as Madeleine Forell Marshall and Janet Todd have misunderstood me.[8] They protest that the congregational hymn was 'an artful composition by literary men in the eighteenth century'. But I never denied this, nor would deny it now; my point was, and is, that the audience to which these poems were addressed have treated these 'artful compositions' as if they were the artless compositions of a communal folk-muse, transmitted orally through generations and in that process continually adapted or transformed. In this respect, *and in no other*, they are like the Border Ballads. The most elegant and least disputatious word for what Montgomery does with Byrom's original is to call it, as Julian does, a *cento*, thereby straining only a little Sir Paul Harvey's definition (in *The Oxford Companion to English Literature*

[8] Madeleine Forell Marshall and Janet Todd, *English Congregational Hymns in the Eighteenth Century* (Lexington, Kentucky, 1982), p. 9.

(1937)): 'a literary composition made up of scraps from various authors, or, more loosely, a "string" or farrago'. But if this device saves the congregational hymn at a pinch for the array of neo-classical genres (and for suitably unimpassioned academic study), it evades the real scandal; which is that, when we study the congregational hymn, we are studying a live genre which is changing even as we study it. It is the *liveness* that disconcerts us. These poems are alive – in tattered hymnals, on insecure music-stands, and in the inexact memories of infrequent worshippers everywhere from London to Kuala Lumpur. This coming Sunday we may be called upon, in church or chapel, to sing a hymn which, if we care to look, our hymnal ascribes to perhaps Isaac Watts; and then we may be instructed from the pulpit to 'omit stanzas two and five'. How can a poem thus brusquely and cavalierly still *in use* be brought into conjunction with poems that on weekdays we discuss in seminar rooms, poems of which the sole use (it sometimes seems) is to provoke such discussions? It is some such inarticulate feeling, we may suspect, that pushes congregational hymns into the margins of literary history.

Byrom, in the system of shorthand that he perfected – that being his chief claim to fame apart from his verses – wrote to Charles Wesley in March, 1738:

I do not at all desire to discourage your publication; but when you tell me that you write not for the critic but for the Christian, it occurs to my mind that you might as well write for both, or in such a manner that the critic may by your writing be moved to turn Christian, rather than the Christian turn critic. I should be wanting, I fear, in speaking freely and friendly upon this matter, if I did not give it as my humble opinion, that before you publish you might lay before some experienced Christian critics, or judges, the design which you are upon; but I speak this with all submission, it is very likely that in these matters I may want a spur more than you want a bridle.[9]

The young Wesley's reply to this courtly but deflating advice has not survived. One would like to think that he civilly protested that the alternatives Byrom put before him are false. He might also have observed that the objective which Byrom recommends – 'that the critic may by your writing be moved to turn Christian' – had already been reached, a quarter-century earlier, by Addison, 'Mr Spectator'.

Addison's is not a name to set pulses racing nowadays. He is by

---

[9] John Byrom, *Remains*, vol. 2, part 1 (1856), p. 196.

common though languid consent a great man and a great writer, but
his greatness, equable and harmonious, is much less to modern taste
than the divided and tormented greatness of a contemporary of his such
as Swift. Least of all is he now esteemed as a poet; though the author of
Cato certainly deserves less shabby treatment. However that may be, the
five sacred poems that Addison composed and printed in *The Spectator* in
1712, are crucial to an understanding of what the congregational hymn
is and how it came about.

The first of them, 'The Lord my Pasture shall prepare', is a poor
thing. The writing is betrayingly adjectival, and the shepherd that it
offers to speak for patently has more to do with *le petit Trianon* than with
the sun-baked uplands of ancient Israel. No one who even half remem-
bers Psalm 23 in the Authorized Version or The Book of Common
Prayer can tolerate Addison's version of it. The interesting question is
why a man so intelligent as Addison, and so conscious of his responsi-
bilities as a public educator, should have miscalculated so grievously.
The reason, we may think, emerges when the version is returned to its
original context, *Spectator* No. 441, published 26 July 1712. There the
verses are appended to an essay 'Divine Providence' (signed 'C') and
are introduced thus:

David has very beautifully represented this steady reliance on God Almighty in
his twenty-third psalm, which is a kind of pastoral hymn, and filled with those
allusions which are usual in that kind of writing. As the poetry is very exquisite,
I shall present my readers with the following translation of it.

Here 'hymn', prefixed by 'pastoral', rather plainly means the Graeco-
Roman genre, not the Hebrew one – still less, therefore, the congregational hymn that Charles Wesley was to make his own. (Even so, it is
hard to see what classical precedent Addison could appeal to, unless it
were Theocritus' Idyll 22, which is a long hymn to the Dioscuri, Castor
and Pollux.) For Addison, we perceive, the Hebrew psalm, so far from
being a genre in its own right, is to be esteemed only when, and so far as,
it can be seen to fall in with some one of the Graeco-Roman genres; and
it is an exercise of taste on the part of the critic to find which of the
classical genres any given psalm can be made to approximate to.

Two weeks later, Addison could do a great deal better:

> When all thy Mercies, O my God,
>   My rising Soul surveys;
> Transported with the View, I'm lost
>   In Wonder, Love, and Praise.

O how shall Words with equal Warmth
    The Gratitude declare
That glows within my Ravish'd Heart!
    But thou canst read it there.

Thy Providence my Life sustain'd
    And all my Wants redrest,
When in the silent Womb I lay,
    And hung upon the Breast.

The piece is sustained through ten more quatrains, and at least one of them is deplorable, but before the end it reaches to an elevation which can still register as a shock:

When Nature fails, and Day and Night
    Divide thy Works no more,
My Ever-grateful Heart, O Lord,
    Thy Mercy shall adore.

In its context, however – *Spectator* No. 453, appended to an essay on 'Gratitude' (signed 'C') – the piece is still prepared for by anxious observations about 'Odes', Greek and Latin as well as Hebrew.[10]

Addison's next sacred poem (*Spectator* No. 465, 23 August 1712) is his most famous, 'The spacious firmament on high'. And comment upon it may be postponed. It had originally an epigraph from Psalm 19: 'The heavens declare the glory of God'; and it was introduced by a prefatory note: 'As such a bold and sublime manner of Thinking furnished out very noble Matter for an Ode, the Reader may see it wrought into the following one.'

Spectator No. 489, for Saturday, 20 September 1712, supplies what is certainly the quaintest of Addison's hymns and, so some may think, in many ways the most appealing. It is not called a hymn, however, but 'a Divine Ode'. It comes after an essay on 'Greatness', making particular reference to the ocean, which reveals Addison's fascination with the then still novel concept of 'the sublime'; and we can be sure that he had not overlooked how 'Longinus', patentee of sublimity, had found that quality pre-eminently in the Hebrew Scriptures:

How are thy Servants blest, O Lord!
    How sure is their Defence!

---

[10] This piece survives into nearly all our hymnals, but never in its entirety. A random check discovers it emasculated to 7 stanzas in *The Church Hymnal for the Christian Year* (1920); to 6 in Ira Sankey's *Sacred Songs and Solos* (n.d.); to 5 in *Hymns for Today's Church* (1982); and 4 in *The Baptist Hymnal* (Nashville, 1975).

Eternal Wisdom is their Guide,
    Their Help Omnipotence.

In foreign Realms, and Lands remote,
    Supported by Thy Care,
Through burning Climes I pass'd unhurt
    And breath'd in tainted Air.

Thy Mercy sweet'ned ev'ry Soil,
    Made ev'ry Region please;
The hoary *Alpine* Hills it warm'd,
    And smoak'd the *Tyrrhene* Seas:

Think, O my Soul, devoutly think,
    How with affrighted Eyes
Thou saw'st the wide extended Deep
    In all its Horrors rise!

Confusion dwelt in ev'ry Face,
    And Fear in ev'ry Heart;
When Waves on Waves, and Gulphs in Gulphs,
    O'ercame the Pilot's Art,

Yet then from all my Griefs, O Lord,
    Thy Mercy set me free,
Whilst in the Confidence of Pray'r
    My Soul took Hold on Thee;

For tho' in dreadful Whirles we hung
    High on the broken Wave,
I knew Thou wert not slow to hear,
    Nor Impotent to save.

The Storm was laid, the Winds retir'd,
    Obedient to Thy Will;
The Sea, that roar'd at Thy Command,
    At Thy Command was still.

In Midst of Dangers, Fears and Death,
    Thy Goodness I'll adore,
And praise Thee for Thy Mercies past;
    And humbly hope for more.

My Life, if Thou preserv'st my Life,
    Thy sacrifice shall be;
And Death, if Death must be my Doom,
    Shall join my Soul to Thee!

This may indeed be an ode; it certainly is not a congregational hymn. It is too personal for that, being apparently a reminiscence of Addison's travels in France and off the Italian coast, 1699–1702; and also it is too narrative. It is only proper that *The Church Hymnal for the Christian Year*, at the same time as it abbreviates the poem to seven stanzas, should eliminate the first person singular throughout, and substitute present tense for past. (On the other hand, only perverted taste could have preferred for line 25 'When by the dreadful tempest borne'.) Charles Wesley, however, could certainly have found in places here the sort of diction he needed, notably in 'The Sea, that roar'd at Thy Command, / At Thy Command was still.'

The only one of these compositions which Addison called unequivocally a hymn was the last of them, 'When rising from the bed of death', in *Spectator* No. 513, Saturday, 18 October 1712. Ironically, this is the one that seems not to have survived into our hymn-books.

There remains 'The spacious firmament on high', of which the third and last stanza runs (speaking of moons, stars and planets):

> What though, in solemn silence, all
> Move round the dark, terrestrial ball?
> What though nor real voice nor sound
> Amid their radiant orbs be found?
> In reason's ear they all rejoice,
> And utter forth a glorious voice,
> For ever singing, as they shine,
> 'The hand that made us is divine'.

These lines are crucial in the history of English devotional poetry in that they confront for the first time the threat to received theological arguments posed by John Locke's demolition of such time-honoured notions as the music of the spheres, and by Locke's more far-reaching argument that 'reality', since it is colourless, soundless, scentless (all such sensuous qualities being 'secondary' and dependent on the observer), must be unimaginable, inhuman and describable only in the abstractions of mathematics. Thus in Addison's poem the 'reason's ear' in which the planets continue to 'rejoice' is above all, if not exclusively, the ear of a mathematician.

Probably too much has been made of the threat that Locke's epistemology posed to poetry as well as to religion. The poet is a sturdier creature, and more resourceful, than is supposed by solicitous historians of ideas like A. N. Whitehead, Basil Willey, Douglas Bush and R. L.

Brett.[11] All the same, Addison can accommodate Locke's arguments only by pushing to the limits the resources of his language. His verses are not in the end defenceless before such coarse-grained questions as 'What sort of ear does Reason have?' or 'How can the human creature hear through any ear but his own?' All the same, it is a rather desperately near-run thing. And there is something at once comical, alarming and touching in the fact that these words are sung confidently, Sunday by Sunday, by congregations unaware that, not only are they assenting to very abstruse cogitations, but they are abetting the most daring of certain rhetorical figures, notably *prosopopoeia*. So far can we be carried out of or beyond ourselves by a melody from Haydn or Walford Davies.

What is certain is that Charles Wesley, though he doubtless knew and had pondered these matters canvassed by Addison, was not going to wrestle with them in his own verses. Though he may not have been sure of it as early as 1738, his subsequent career shows him holding by the intention he had declared to Byrom: 'to write not for the critic but for the Christian'. This may be disputed. In 1757 John Wesley, triumphing in the success of the Methodists' singing, echoed and endorsed Byrom's formulation, which by then it seems had become a rhetorical commonplace:

When it is seasonable to sing praise to GOD they do it with the spirit and with the understanding also; not in the miserable, scandalous doggerel of Hopkins and Sternhold, but in psalms and hymns which are both sense and poetry, such as would sooner dispose a critic to turn Christian than a Christian to turn critic.

But John Wesley, though a very adroit promoter of his brother's poetry, is for just that reason not always reliable in the accounts he gives of it. The brothers, it is well known, did not always see eye to eye nor speak with one voice; and Charles Wesley's sacred poems differ from Addison's much more widely than his brother chooses to acknowledge. Not only are Wesley's hymns *congregational* in a way that, as we have seen, Addison's are not, but the congregations that he wrote them for were of a sort that neither Addison nor Byrom in 1738 could have envisaged: open-air field meetings, with no liturgical structure beyond what the evangelist improvised as he went on. Mr Locke's epistemology was not a matter that could be broached to any purpose in those contexts, and hardly one of the evangelist's hearers on such an occasion would have

[11] See R. L. Brett, *The Third Earl of Shaftesbury. A Study in Eighteenth-Century Literary Theory* (1951), p. 14.

thought of himself as a 'critic'. Charles Wesley's devotional poetry was radically new in ways that his brother either did not recognize or else found it prudent to conceal.

This is not to say, however, that the fervours and fevers of Count Zinzendorf and his Moravians, once they had been naturalized by the astonishing joint genius of the Wesley brothers, show up Addison's piety as a pallid imitation of 'the real thing'. Addison's piety, we must think, was thoroughly genuine, and of a sort that will always quite properly appeal to minds of a certain cast. Byrom, whom we may judge to have been Addisonian to the end of his life, caught the flavour and the fragrance of it very well when he wrote to his sister in 1729 from London:

But, for Mr. Law, and Christian religion, and such things, they are mightily out of fashion at present; indeed I do not wonder at it, for it is a plain, calm business, and here people are, and love to be, all of a hurry, and to talk their philosophy, their vain philosophy, in which they agree with one another in nothing but rejecting many received opinions.[12]

Remembering how important to the Wesleyan as to subsequent evangelists is the thunder-clap of 'conversion', experienced as abrupt, violent and all-transforming, we may value even more a reflection that Byrom that same year confided to his Journal: 'When truth rises in the mind at first it makes a long shadow, but when it is vertical, and shines perpendicularly through us, little or no shadow.'[13] Byrom's faith, like Addison's, casts few shadows, and those short; that does not make it any the less authentic, and we go very wrong if we suppose that those for whom Christianity is 'a plain, calm business' are Erastians, or Deists in thin disguise.

[12] John Byrom, *Remains*, vol. 1, part 2 (1855), p. 328.
[13] *ibid.*, p. 367.

2

Isaac Watts: the axiomatic hymns

The word 'fundamentalist', as commonly used to distinguish certain religious groupings from others (inside for instance Islam as well as Christendom), may be perilously misleading. All religions are fundamentalist to the extent that they all – leaving aside self-deluders and self-intoxicators on the fringes – declare certain propositions and professions to be fundamental, as distinct from others that are optional and debatable. The *fundamental* formulations ('fundamental' meaning 'on the bottom line') are those that a person must assent to if he or she is to subscribe himself or herself, Christian or Mohammedan or whatever else. If a person continue to profess Christianity or Mohammedanism while refusing such assent, he or she offends not against authoritarian edicts but against *reason*; he or she is, in the language of the laws about consumer trading, offering a product (himself or herself) under a fraudulent and misleading label. However sincere the avowal, it is a false 'trade-description'.

Effectively then, inside any religious communion the fundamentalists are distinct only in so far as they discern, and try to demand, relatively many such fundamental tenets, whereas others deemed more moderate or liberal discern relatively few. Though at the extreme liberal end of the spectrum are to be found some who delude themselves that no tenet at all is truly fundamental, it remains true that within Christendom as within Islam the difference between fundamentalists and the rest is a difference only of emphasis and degree.

The proper name for such tenets alleged to be fundamental is *dogmata*. But because 'dogmatic' has for a long time been treated illegitimately as a term of abuse, it has to be pointed out that 'dogmatic' means nothing more nor less than 'axiomatic'. And it may be questioned whether there is or can be any human thinking that is not axiomatic in the sense that it must take as its starting-point one or more axioms such as 'A thing cannot both be and not be at the same time.'

But that is a question for philosophers and logicians; what is certain is that religious thinking – the thinking for instance of a professing and believing Christian – is and cannot help but be, unashamedly, axiomatic. The axioms in question may be many or few, according as the thinker is more or less 'fundamentalist'. But axiomatic his thinking must be, in the nature of the case.

It is from this perception that we must rule out of court the complaint made against Isaac Watts that he is an *axiomatic* thinker. The objection was raised by John Hoyles in his *The Waning of the Renaissance 1640–1740* (Martinus Nijhoff, The Hague, 1971), a work which in other ways champions Watts and in particular establishes him as an intellectual presence in his time and for long after, more than just a hymn-writer. To be sure, Hoyles does not single out Watts for condemnation, but includes in the indictment George Berkeley, Bishop of Cloyne, and even Henry St John, Viscount Bolingbroke:

> The belief that truth can be expressed axiomatically is characteristic of the English Enlightenment. This belief reflects a timidity and prudence with regard to the intellect, and a common refusal to raise the ghost of seventeenth century controversy. Indeed one could argue that England had had her Enlightenment under Cromwell, when Hobbes and Milton had written for and about the absolutist mind, and the foundations of the Royal Society had been laid. But England had thrown overboard the political and religious dimensions of this Enlightenment, and severely reduced the scope of its cultural and intellectual implications. The eighteenth century suffered accordingly, and Watts voices its ethos.

Such rating down of the eighteenth century by comparison with the seventeenth has been common ever since Leslie Stephen. What we may notice with dismay in this modern reformulation is seeing 'prudence' linked with 'timidity'; and also the sleight of hand by which 'absolutist' – a term from political history and political theory (in which sense it is clearly apposite to both Milton and Hobbes) – is extended to intellectual history ('the absolutist *mind*') and in that sense is unequivocally approved. Neither Hobbes nor Milton was a prudent thinker, and the more credit to them, for this saved them from being timid; such seems to be Hoyles' argument.

Elsewhere he writes (p. 153): 'Watts's argument for Enlightenment is not so much based on the clarifying energy of intellectual vision, as on the axiomatic propositions of a social and religious compromise.' And again (p. 183): 'the puritan insistence on the uses of reason was obsolete in an age which formulated its truths in axioms; and Watts himself spent a lot of time speaking the language of axiomatic theology'. But as we have seen it is inconceivable how any theology can be other than 'axiomatic'. And at the level of common sense it is hard to see how not to applaud as simply prudent certain passages that Hoyles cites to exemplify the cravenly axiomatic and timid. From Berkeley, for instance, in *Alciphron, or The Minute Philosopher* (1732):

Errors and nonsense, as such, are of small concern in the eye of the public, which considereth not the metaphysical truth of notions, so much as the tendency they have to produce good or evil. Truth itself is valued by the public, as it hath an influence, and is felt in the course of life. You may confute a whole shelf of Schoolmen, and discover many speculative truths, without any great merit towards your country. (J. Hoyles, *The Waning of the Renaissance 1640–1740*, p. 173)

Or there is Watts himself, in his *Philosophical Essays*:

Let our reason blush and hide its head, and lie abased for ever at the foot of the divine majesty. This strange theatre of argument, this endless war of words and ideas, throws a world of confusion and abasement upon the proudest powers of mankind. (J. Hoyles, *The Waning of the Renaissance 1640–1740*, p. 187)

And finally there is, for good measure, the anti-clerical and perhaps infidel Bolingbroke:

The phenomena of the human mind are few, and on these few a multitude of hypotheses have been raised, concerning mind in general, and soul or spirit. So that in this part, the improvement of real knowledge must be made by contraction, and not by amplification. (J. Hoyles, *The Waning of the Renaissance 1640–1740*, p. 156)

We may be not unstirred by John Hoyles' clarion-call to 'the clarifying energy of intellectual vision'. But if we want to take the force of Watts' vision – and of Berkeley's, even of Bolingbroke's – we have to accustom ourselves to less heady perspectives, in which for instance prudence is a cardinal virtue.

It is that more prudent ethos which – necessarily indeed, since Dissenters under Charles II had been harried and persecuted – presided over, and sustained through many generations, the Dissenting Academies. These have been admiringly documented, except for those numerous ones which for good and pressing reasons kept no records. But there has been a reluctance to consider this evidence outside the specialized discipline of the History of Education; plainly what the academies represent is something of more generally cultural significance. And Watts' career, more than any other, compels that recognition.

Historians of the academies – not excluding the exceptionally scrupulous and fair-minded Padraig O'Brien[1] – are reluctant to admit the possibility that the cultural enterprise which the academies represent came to its peak quite early, with if not before Philip Doddridge's Northampton academy (1729–50). The later academies, at Hackney for instance and notably at Warrington (1757–86), provide the names that achieved a more than sectarian lustre: Joseph Priestley, Jean Paul Marat, William Godwin, Gilbert Wakefield. Yet these later academies inculcated both theological laxity (Socinian, becoming Unitarian), and a corresponding laxity about socio-political responsibility (disaffection, becoming Jacobin). It may be that the truly heroic names in what was indeed a heroic enterprise came earlier, and are seldom remembered: Richard Frankland of the Rathmell academy in Ribblesdale (1669–95), the Welshman Charles Owen of the Sankey Street academy in Warrington, Peter Aspinwall (d. 1696), John Jennings of the Kibworth academy (1688–1723) and others.

Watts founded no academy, though he may have been the moving spirit behind Doddridge's. But his extra-curricular influence as an educator cannot be doubted. A striking instance is the case of Michael Faraday (1791–1867). Faraday's modern biographer, Joseph Agassi (*Faraday as a Natural Philosopher*, 1971), is revealing:

Perhaps I should mention that Dr. Isaac Watts, now scarcely remembered, and then as a pompous eighteenth-century hymn-writer, was once the authority on self-improvement, on studying, on keeping the mind open and free of prejudice, on learning from experience, and so on. Faraday's earliest publication is a small lecture he gave in his twenties, exclusively based on Watts, about means of learning: from observation, from reading, from conversations with people – about their own knowledge, about commonly interesting topics, and so on.

Faraday's textbook in fact was Watts' *Improvement of the Mind* (1741), of which Samuel Johnson wrote: 'Whoever has the care of instructing others, may be charged with deficience in his duty if this book is not recommended.' Plainly the great scientist thought that he had been enlightened by Watts, and this vindicates John Hoyles in supposing that Watts was, for good or ill, a luminary of the Enlightenment. Joseph Agassi, though he cannot discount the evidence, gives every sign of finding it hard to believe. And he probably speaks for the majority; for on the most commonly received understanding of the Enlightenment, priests and ministers, evangelists and hymn-singers are certainly outside

[1] Padraig O'Brien, *Warrington Academy 1757–86. Its Predecessors and Successors* (Wigan, 1989).

its pale. As enthusiastically taken over and patented by Marxists and other atheists, indeed by agnostic 'liberals', the Enlightenment signifies a period – mostly (though this is left vague) in the eighteenth century – when western man, liberating himself from hitherto unquestioned axioms, was able thereby to uncover crucial truths in political science and also in the natural sciences. In fact, we have found reason to think the only axioms that were – for a few people – overturned and discredited were those of institutional Christianity, the *dogmata*; other axioms flourished and were credited as perhaps never before.

Joseph Agassi's epithet for Watts as hymnist is 'pompous'. It may be doubted whether he came on the word after long consideration, or out of a persevering engagement with Watts' verse-writings. After all, Agassi is a historian of science, not of poetry. Yet there is evidence that throughout the nineteenth century and certainly up to our own day 'pompous' – an alternative word is 'stilted' – does point to an obstruction that reasonably well-intentioned readers encounter, and are repelled by, when they try to engage with Watts' poems and hymns in cold print, without the adventitious easements of music, communal amity and ecclesiastical setting. The difficulty, since it is a real one for many people, must be confronted.

The first thing to observe is that the same impediment arises with the secular verse of Watts' period as with the sacred. Alexander Pope, because when he wishes he can handle the colloquial and comic registers of English as well as the elevated, is something of a special case. Dryden is a more telling instance, and a dispiriting one; for there is abundant evidence that the greatness of Dryden's poetry – as apparent in his verse-translations as in his original poems – is obscured for many readers because he characteristically (not universally) pitches his tone of address too high for their comfort. What we have to deal with, alas, appears to be a change in sensibility so radical, and now through many generations so often enforced, that it is for many people irreversible. The affectation, or the rhetorical illusion, that the poet speaks 'from the heart', nakedly, is now for many readers so inextricable from their experience of poetry that they cannot make contact with poets like Dryden or Watts for whom that affectation or rhetorical illusion is undesirable and uninteresting.

We return here, surely, to that feature of Watts' writing, whether in verse or prose, that John Hoyles defined and castigated as 'axiomatic'. Since the truths of the Christian Revelation are axiomatic, there is no need – and indeed it would be impertinent – for them to be, in the words of a Romantic poet, 'proved on the pulses'. An axiom is just that, axiomatic; it does not have to be re-experienced, not in poetry nor anywhere else except (ideally) in the act of worship. To push the matter a little further, for Christian poets like Dryden and Watts, poetry is distinctly *not* worship, though it may be an adjunct to worship or a component of it.

It is within some such barely recoverable frame of reference that we must try to engage with Watts' 'Hosanna to the Royal Son':

> Hosanna to the royal son
>> Of David's ancient line!
> His natures two, his person one,
>> Mysterious and divine.
>
> The root of David, here we find,
>> And offspring, are the same:
> Eternity and time are joined
>> In our Immanuel's name.
>
> Blest he that comes to wretched man
>> With peaceful news from Heaven!
> Hosannas, of the highest strain,
>> To Christ the Lord be given.
>
> Let mortals ne'er refuse to take
>> Th' Hosanna on their tongues;
> Lest rocks and stones should rise, and break
>> Their silence into songs.

There are readers with whom it will cut no ice when they are asked to admire the sinewy intellectualism of this poem – the compressed wit which expresses the paradox of Jesus belonging at once to Eternity and to Time by saying that in him 'The root of David . . . And offspring, are the same.' This they are likely to dismiss as mere cleverness, adroit indeed but unfeeling. Augustus Toplady, reprinting Watts' hymn (in *Psalms and Hymns for Public and Private Worship*, 1776), allowed for Wesleyan and evangelical sensibilities by substituting for the last quatrain:

> Should we, dear Lord, refuse to take
>> The Hosanna on our tongues,
> The rocks and stones would rise and break
>> Their silence into songs.

The changes seem minor, and yet they are crucial. For Toplady, the supposed behaviour of the stones is hyperbolical, allowing him to harangue his readers reproachfully: 'You feel so little that even stones would feel more.' But for Watts, the stones' supposed behaviour is simply the necessary consequence of the axiom: if God is the Creator, then every one of His creatures – stones as well as men – responds to Him and moves at His command. This is clearer if we refer to the scriptural passage behind the hymn – as Watts directs that we should, for the hymn is in Book I of his *Hymns and Spiritual Songs*, among the hymns specifically described as 'collected from the holy scriptures'. In the text from Luke that provides the 'Benedictus' in *The Book of Common Prayer*, a distinction is made between the Creator, God the Father, described as 'the Lord', and God the Son, described as 'the King':

Saying, Blessed bee the King that commeth in the Name of the Lord, peace in heaven, and glory in the Highest.

Watts cleaves very faithfully, as Toplady does not, to Luke's account of the relevant episode (Luke 19.37–40):

And when he was come nigh even now at the descent of the mount of Olives, the whole multitude of the disciples began to rejoyce and praise God with a loud voice, for all the mighty workes that they had seene,

Saying, Blessed bee the King that commeth in the Name of the Lord, peace in heaven, and glory in the Highest.

And some of the Pharisees from among the multitude saide unto him, Master, rebuke thy disciples.

And he answered, and said unto them, I tell you, that if these should holde their peace, the stones would immediately cry out.

Jesus here can hardly be boasting to the pharisees about the lately demonstrated fervour of his disciples; he is declaring on the contrary that, even were his human creatures deficient in fervour, he could call on his inhuman creatures, like rocks and stones, to witness for him or for the Lord in whose name he comes. The quality of human response is neither here nor there. Similarly God the Son and King is 'blessed', whether or not he is apprehended as 'dear'. The quality or intensity of the worshippers' response is for Watts irrelevant: the omnipotence of the triune God – Father, Son and Holy Spirit – has to be acknowledged; it need not be 'experienced'. Thus Watts' declaration is axiomatic in being scriptural – the truth of the Revelation persists, whether or not human beings acknowledge it. In fact, the most that can be asked of them is that they acknowledge it; to not just acknowledge but *experience* it, is something that Toplady would exact, but Watts does not.

Not many of Watts' hymns are so sternly axiomatic as this. And those which are, are not among the best loved or most often used in worship.

Yet the same uncompromising note is struck even when Watts is more confiding, using for instance the first person plural:

> 'Tis God, who lifts our comforts high,
>   Or sinks them in the grave;
> He gives – and (blessed be his name!)
>   He takes but what he gave.
>
> Peace, all our angry passions, then,
>   Let each rebellious sigh
> Be silent at his sovereign will,
>   And every murmur die.
>
> If smiling mercy crown our lives,
>   Its praises shall be spread;
> And we'll adore the justice too,
>   That strikes our comforts dead.

It is very difficult for a modern reader, however devout, not to hear in the severity of that last line a sort of vindictive satisfaction. And yet, once again, the position is axiomatic: the Christian cannot delight in God's mercy (the Second Person of the Trinity) without delighting also in His justice (the First Person). 'Delight in' may well seem hardly the right expression. And sure enough Watts provides the right one, 'adore' – which as Watts uses it here (and elsewhere) is by no means simply an intensive variant on 'love'. We love what we can understand; we adore what passes understanding – that seems to be Watts' position. And no doubt a competent theologian could say whether this too is not axiomatic.

   Watts at the end of his life was suspected of having Arian leanings. But at the time he wrote these poems, he was firmly and insistently Trinitarian. If we are right so far, he could hardly be anything else. Accordingly he composed no less than sixteen doxologies, grouping them together at the end of his *Hymns and Spiritual Songs*, and drawing attention to them with a special brief introduction:

I cannot persuade myself to put a full period to these Divine Hymns, until I have expressed a special Song of Glory to God the Father, the Son, and the Holy Spirit. Though the Latin name of it, Gloria Patri, be retained in the *English* nation from the *Roman* Church; and though there may be some excesses of superstitious honour paid to the words of it, which may have wrought some unhappy prejudices in weaker Christians; yet I believe it still to be one of the noblest parts of Christian Worship. The subject of it is the doctrine of the Trinity, which is that peculiar Glory of the Divine Nature, that our Lord Jesus

Christ has so clearly revealed unto men, and is so necessary to true Christianity. The action is Praise; which is one of the most complete and exalted parts of heavenly worship. I have cast the Song into a variety of forms, and have fitted it, by a plain Version, or a larger Paraphrase, to be sung either alone, or at the conclusion of another Hymn.

It is not altogether clear whether the doxology numbered as Hymn 29 in Book III of *Hymns and Spiritual Sons* would be considered by Watts 'a plain version' or 'a larger paraphrase':

> Glory to God the Trinity,
> Whose name has mysteries unknown:
> In essence One, in persons Three;
> A social nature, yet alone.
>
> When all our noblest powers are join'd,
> The honours of thy name to raise;
> Thy glories overmatch our mind,
> And angels faint beneath the praise.

The quaint but real elegance of 'A social nature, yet alone' will not qualify for most modern readers as 'plain'; and accordingly these verses are probably not apt for modern devotional use, though as poetry they are delightful. However that may be, Watts' implication is as before: it is when our minds are 'overmatched', that we can only *adore* (as angels do). And what we then adore is not God's goodness nor His power, not His mercy nor His justice, but His Glory – which binds together all His other attributes in a combination we can apprehend but not explain. What is striking is not so much Watts' readiness to value pre-Reformation and Romish practices, as his use of words like 'noblest' and 'honours' and 'exalted'. However it was in earlier Dissenting generations and in other Dissenting communions in his day, it is clear that for his Congregationalists about 1707 to be 'plain' did not mean to be inelegant, unadorned or scrupulously mean. To that extent when later readers find Watts 'pompous', the pomp they discern is truly there, and intended. As his biographer Harry Escott reminds us, the Dissenting circles that Watts moved in were 'stately and learned'.

However, Watts' understanding of the Holy Trinity, at least as we know it through his verse, is curiously deficient in one respect: nowhere does he firmly delineate the nature and office of the Third Person. In his as in most doxologies the Holy Spirit tends to bring up the rear as a pious afterthought. But in his less constricted hymns the case is the same. And if there is question of the Enlightenment, this is betraying;

for in orthodox interpretations it is the Holy Spirit that illuminates, that
enlightens. To be sure, in Hymn 133 of Watts' Book II we read:

> Eternal Spirit, we confess
> And sing the wonders of thy grace ...
>
> Enlighten'd by thy heavenly ray,
> Our shades and darkness turn to day ...

But this phrasing is in no way compelling. (It is what we may suspect
some readers will call 'axiomatic', though the right word for it, surely, is
'formulaic'.) Elsewhere Watts treats the Holy Ghost in images not of
light but fire:

> Come, Holy Spirit, heavenly Dove,
>   With all thy quick'ning powers, –
> Kindle a flame of sacred love
>   In these cold hearts of ours.

It is hard to read anything axiomatic out of this; it seems to appeal only
for greater fervour, quite in the manner of Toplady. It is seventy years
later, with Cowper, that we find the Holy Spirit conceived, and
pursued consistently, through images of light breaking:

> The Spirit breathes upon the Word,
>   And brings the truth to sight;
> Precepts and promises afford
>   A sanctifying light.
>
> A glory gilds the sacred page,
>   Majestic like the sun;
> It gives a light to every age,
>   It gives, but borrows none.
>
> The hand that gave it still supplies
>   The gracious light and heat;
> His truths upon the nations rise,
>   They rise, but never set.
>
> Let everlasting thanks be thine
>   For such a bright display
> As makes a world of darkness shine
>   With beams of heavenly day.
>
> My soul rejoices to pursue
>   The steps of him I love,
> Till glory breaks upon my view
>   In brighter words above.

On this showing Watts certainly seems more reluctant that Cowper to trust what John Howles calls 'the clarifying energy of intellectual vision'; less confident, in other words, that that clarifying energy is the Holy Spirit in action.

Cowper, as always, speaks from experience – his own. He has perused Holy Writ to no purpose many times; he knows the Holy Spirit, and praises him, for the times when on the contrary the Writ spoke to him. This is possible for Cowper because he speaks from the pew, unlike Watts or Cowper's collaborator John Newton who speak from the pulpit, and are accordingly axiomatic, as Cowper neither needs nor wants to be.

However, we must surely beware of supposing that Cowper represents an advance on Watts, whether religiously or poetically – just as we must avoid the opposite temptation, a historical relativism that says Watts was right in and for his time, as Cowper was right in and for his. To appeal from and to experience in these matters is not inherently better, or more honest, than to appeal from and to axioms. Nevertheless, though the difference between Cowper's treatment and Watts' cannot be construed as an advance, it certainly marks a change, and a momentous one. No statement of that change is at once so sweeping and so succinct as Ian Watt's:

> The thought of the past, from Plato and Augustine to Aquinas and Spinoza, had assumed some form of the view that truth was eternal, changeless, and unified, and that therefore the particular experiences of the individual in the temporal world of change were illusory or merely contingent, and certainly gave no reliable access to reality or truth. This dualism of the eternal and the temporal orders was strongly challenged by the empirical and scientific movements associated with the names of Locke and Newton, and as a result man and his world came increasingly to be understood as the results of a temporal process: in their different ways Darwin, Marx, and Freud all suggested that the individual life must be understood in the context of a process of chronological development – biological, economic, or psychic.[2]

There is no doubt that among the names invoked here, Watts belongs with Plato and Augustine, Aquinas and Spinoza. It is less easy to see Cowper in the company of Darwin, Marx and Freud, particularly since he was at least as much a Calvinist as Watts was. And yet he does belong with them, rather than with Watts or Spinoza. For as we know, Cowper could square his Calvinist belief with his mature and harrowing

[2] Ian Watt, *Conrad in the Nineteenth Century* (1979), p. 288.

experience only by the desperate expedient of maintaining that God had made in his case a unique and horrifying exception, withdrawing from him the salvation that had once been granted. Thus God's purposes, supposedly eternal and changeless, are alleged by Cowper to have changed in the course of time, in the course of one human lifetime, his own. And that life, he thus came to believe, 'must be understood in the context of a process of chronological development'.

Of course it is possible to think that the desperateness of Cowper's expedient shows how Watts' Calvinism had become, by Cowper's time, unthinkable for honest and intelligent people. And if so, how much less tenable it must be for us, post-Darwinian, post-Marxian, post-Freudian! Deeply insulting though it is to those who still profess Calvinism, as to the many more who conceive themselves to profess the faith of Augustine and Aquinas, this argument has been voiced so often that it is in some circles a commonplace. Religious belief, it has been bluntly said, is irreconcilable with 'the modern mind'. But even if that were so in some general and abstract sense, it is quite clear that the most modern mind, if (perhaps perversely) it chooses to set itself the task, *can* still enter the imaginative world of Watts, the world of the axiom. One way to make that passage is by relishing the literary (aesthetic) pleasures that only the world of the axiomatic can supply. If this seems like connoisseurship, the murmurous satisfaction of the antiquary, so be it; perhaps connoisseurship and antiquarianism deserve better than the obloquy that is commonly heaped on them. The connoisseur of poetic diction will, if he pursues that preoccupation strenuously enough, break out of the world of 'the aesthetic' into regions of human experience more liberating, though also more alarming.

3

Watts' atrocity hymns

No hymn by Watts – not even 'Our God, our help in ages past' – is
better known or more loved than 'When I survey the wondrous cross':

> When I survey the wondrous cross
> On which the Prince of glory dy'd,
> My richest gain I count but loss,
> And pour contempt on all my pride.
>
> Forbid it, Lord, that I should boast,
> Save in the death of Christ, my God:
> – All the vain things that charm me most
> I sacrifice them to his blood.
>
> See from his head, his hands, his feet,
> Sorrow and love flow mingled down!
> Did e'er such love and sorrow meet
> Or thorns compose so rich a crown!
>
> His dying crimson, like a robe,
> Spreads o'er his body on the tree;
> – Then am I dead to all the globe,
> And all the globe is dead to me.
>
> Were the whole realm of nature mine,
> That were a present far too small;
> Love so amazing, so divine,
> Demands my soul, my life, my all.

The word is 'survey'; not 'behold' nor 'discern', not 'observe' nor
'perceive'. 'Survey' is the word also at the start of Johnson's *Vanity of
Human Wishes* (1749):

> Let Observation with extensive view
> Survey mankind from China to Peru ...

The distrustful wag who translated this as 'let observation with extensive observation observe' had not allowed for the nicety of Johnson the lexicographer. And in Watts' usage too the rightness of 'survey' can be appreciated only if we consult the dictionary. The *Oxford English Dictionary* gives under 'survey':

To look at from, or as from, a height or commanding position; to take a broad, general, or comprehensive view of; to view or examine in its whole extent. *b, fig.* To take a comprehensive mental view of; to consider or contemplate as a whole.

Ever since George Whitefield in 1757 the fourth stanza has habitually been omitted, and the reason for that seems to have everything to do with 'survey' understood too loosely.

For one sees the point of the excision well enough: Watts' 'crimson . . . robe' quite flagrantly refuses to consider the pus and the sweat, the scab and the coagulation and the stink; not to speak of the thronging multitude, its jeerings and gawkings, its horse-laughs or worse. But 'survey' has signalled in advance that these actualities will be ignored: the crucifixion is to be looked at 'from, or as from, a height or commanding position', from which the sweat cannot be smelt, the horse-laughs cannot be heard.

So it is also in the Scripture that Watts is working from: 'But God forbid that I should glory, save in the Crosse of our Lord Jesus Christ, by whom the world is crucified unto me, and I unto the world.' Paul cannot be expostulating to the backsliding Galatians that he 'glories in' the stink and the scab and the horse-laughs; the outlandish English construction, 'crucified unto' (not 'for' nor 'by', but 'unto') could doubtless be explained to us by a student of Pauline Greek. Lacking such help, we can only suppose that by Paul, as by Watts keeping the faith centuries later, the Crucifixion is seen, is 'surveyed', across a vast aesthetic and conceptual distance. A poetics that distrusts, and indeed cannot explain, aesthetic distance falls in with an evangelical piety that distrusts and cannot explain conceptual distance. Both of them – the poetics and the piety – want to 'rub our noses in it'; whereas both Paul and Watts are determined we shall do no such thing. A poetics of 'immediacy' cannot, any more than a theology of 'immediacy', find room for either of them.

To press this home we can consider an admirable treatment of the Crucifixion by a modern poet, W. H. Auden's in 'The Shield of Achilles':

> Barbed wire enclosed an arbitrary spot
> Where bored officials lounged (one cracked a joke)

And sentries sweated, for the day was hot:
    A crowd of ordinary decent folk
    Watched from without and neither moved nor spoke
As three pale figures were led forth and bound
To three posts driven upright in the ground.

The mass and majesty of this world, all
    That carries weight and always weighs the same
Lay in the hands of others; they were small
    And could not hope for help and no help came:
    What their foes liked to do was done, their shame
Was all the worst could wish; they lost their pride
And died as men before their bodies died.

Auden's treatment of the Crucifixion is sharp and moving. It may even be thought by some readers superior to Watts' treatment. But let no one suppose that it is more *immediate*. If recent literary theory, so largely frivolous and self-promoting, has been useful in any way at all, it has been by underlining the fact, never denied but constantly evaded, that nothing comes to us through art except as *mediated* through art; that 'the immediate' is accordingly in art a will o' the wisp, an *ignis fatuus* that recedes before us however far we go. In art, whether verbal or non-verbal, everything is mediated – through the medium that is that art's special conveyance. The nearer art comes to 'the particulars', the more it is prey to the contingent, including the historically contingent. Thus Auden's poem of 1952 is already dated. What we have learned since then of the attitude of a television public towards atrocities suggests that 'neither moved nor spoke' is quite inaccurate; the image we need on the contrary is of motor-cars crawling bumper to bumper through a tail-back of many miles, chivvied indeed by traffic police but leniently because they are impelled by what is thought to be 'natural curiosity', and in any case each car-full represents a 'family outing'. Accordingly Auden's treatment of the Crucifixion is seen to be as stylized, as far from immediate, as Watts'. And indeed Auden, alluding rather plainly to politically enforced 'judicial murders' of the 1930s and 1940s, seems to have recognized this and provided for it.

    Yet Watts' poem is still disconcerting. For the stanza that we suppress seems strikingly and quite uncharacteristically disjointed. What, after all, is the point in time that is defined by 'Then' at the start of its third line? The only way to make sense of it is to relate it back – in defiance of all the punctuation of intervening verses – to the first word of the poem, 'When'. On this showing, it is only when the survey is completed –

when it is, as it must aim to be, comprehensive – that we can be (temporarily no doubt) 'dead to all the globe', 'crucified ... unto the world'.

Very interesting from this point of view is the word 'compose' in line 12: 'Or thorns compose so rich a crown'. In Watts' day 'composure' and 'composition' lay very close together; Philip Doddridge spoke of his hymns as his 'composures'. And for us too the common root must be allowed its force. We may well be shocked at the notion that any one should regard the Crucifixion composedly, with composure; yet the dictionary (once again) compels us to recognize that the attainment of such composure is one necessary aspect of making a satisfactory artistic composition that has the Crucifixion for its subject. What the dictionary inescapably documents as the attitude of our ancestors on this excruciating topic is borne out by testimonies and speculations in modern aesthetics which maintain, with impressive logic, that the atrociousness of such a subject (the event supposedly recorded) is always, *and must be*, dissolved away entirely into the delicious felicities of the medium – into Annibale Carracci's colours and contours and brush-strokes, into Watts' choice diction, his cadences, his rhymes. This perception is the source of the not uncommon protestation that modern atrocities signalled by names like Auschwitz must be declared off limits to artists – since to regard Auschwitz with composure is humanly inexcusable. Yet artists continue trying to comprehend Auschwitz in their art, just as they continue trying to comprehend that prototype (for Christians) of all atrocities, the crucifixion of God made man. If we are honest with ourselves, it is precisely the atrociousness that grips us and spellbinds us – a less atrocious subject would not hold our attention so rapt.

If we agree to that, we are faced with a range of choices: none appealing, some appalling. One of the least appealing explanations is that we exult in art, we triumph in it vicariously, when we see it making beauty out of what is most brutal and squalid. It would be rash to deny that there are – and not just in modern times – artists and connoisseurs of whom this is a true account. The trouble with it is, obviously, that it gives the aesthete and even the artist a vested interest in the brutal and the perverted, in preserving and perpetuating them, since they present our arts with their most challenging occasions. A less ignominious explanation – so it will seem to some, though by no means to all – is that we value these atrocious occasions for the challenge they pose not to our sensibility but to our understanding, not to our art-making but to our conceptualizing. To *understand* these occasions, and even the necessity of them, is different from surmounting and domesticating them. An artist like Watts – and there were relatively many of them in his era, as we shall see – can do the second thing, can seem to 'prettify'; but he can also do the first thing, simultaneously and by the same means. When that happens, art is seen to be, along with much else, an *intellectual* achievement. And that is what we can see Watts achieving; but only if we fly in the face of many generations, and insist on restoring to the poem its fourth stanza.

There remains the problem of the disjointedness, not to say the grammatical disorder. For us to relate the 'Then' of the fifteenth line back to the 'When' of the first, we have to consider most of the intervening lines as a distraught parenthesis. And Watts' practice elsewhere (he, the logician!) gives us no warrant for such a manoeuvre. He of all poets is least likely to have embraced the modern heresy of 'imitative form', according to which the poet expresses distraction (his being distraught) by writing distractedly.

The best solution comes from considering more closely his scriptural source. Paul's Epistle to the Galatians is one of the most impassioned and personal texts in the New Testament. For Galatians 6.11 *The New Oxford Annotated Bible* gives: 'See with what large letters I am writing to you with my own hand,' and the editors comment that this is 'bitterly satirical'. Certainly it seems that in this letter Paul is bitter; wounded and disappointed, and fighting back. So 'God forbid that I should glory, save in the Crosse of our Lord Jesus Christ' is not a pious commonplace, but fighting talk, from one with his back to the wall. Watts expects us, or some of us, to bring that scriptural context to bear – so as to hear in his asseveration not imperturbable assurance but on the contrary desperation. What else indeed, what but desperation, could have provoked from him those exclamatory lines that subsequent generations have found indigestible?

> His dying crimson, like a robe,
> Spreads o'er his body on the tree;
> – Then am I dead to all the globe,
> And all the globe is dead to me.

The 'tree' is as remote from the pegged together baulks of timber, as 'dying crimson, like a robe' is from the blood coagulated or trickling. Both usages, if we attend to them, confirm that the purpose of the verses, their desperate endeavour, is to raise the atrocious occurrence to the level of a concept, a level on which it can be comprehended, with hard-won composure. After all it is only 'in the abstract' that the Cross (any cross) can be conceived of as a 'tree'. Yet the antiquity of the trope suggests that such abstracting, such conceptualizing, was familiar and sought after through many centuries before Isaac Watts. And yet this is an enterprise so alien, if not to modern poetry then to commentators on that poetry, that for these verses to have survived at all into modern memory, however imperfectly, seems not much short of miraculous.

'Aesthetic distance' is a formulation that was sufficiently bandied about not many years ago. But 'conceptual distance' is something new-fangled, which cannot be justified by established usage. And indeed it is only an awkward device for obviating or postponing the one right word: 'idealize'. Watts *idealizes* the Crucifixion, not in the sense that he prettifies it or denies its monstrousness, but in the sense, etymologically correct, that he raises the monstrosity to the level of *idea*. As we have seen, he signals that such is his intention when he announces that he 'surveys' the Cross, not beholds it in his imagination, still less vicariously experiences it. Such idealizing, in that strict sense, was common in his generation and through several before him. Annibale Carracci of Bologna painted Saint Lucy presenting her eyes to the Blessed Virgin; and in his painting the objects that Saint Lucy proffers on a salver are as far from blood-bespattered blobs of jelly as Watts' 'crimson robe' is from the actuality of what Jesus looked like as he hung on the Cross.[1] The trouble that we have in making this connection derives from our preconception that the baroque, a vehicle of the Roman Counter-Reformation, could not have been available to an heir of Cromwellian puritanism like Watts. But the evidence to the contrary is there, in Watts' poems; and if one looks for external evidence, it is to be found in the documented fact of Watts' indebtedness to 'the Christian Horace', the Polish Jesuit writing in Latin, Matthew Casimire Sarbiewski (1595–1640). Odd as it must seem, the idealizing and yet sensuously saturated art of the Counter-Reformation found one of its finest expressions in English in a sacred poem by a nonconformist pastor.

In its disjointedness, whether artfully intended or (more probably, we may think) forced on the poet by the ardour of his meditations, 'When I survey the wondrous cross' seems to stand alone. If this poem is

---

[1] Since the legend of St Lucy rather obviously derives from a pun on her name (Lucy/Lux/ Light), Carracci's picture, like other compositions on the same theme, can be seen as controverting in advance the vaunts to be made by, and on behalf of, 'the Enlightenment'.

baroque, the greater number of Watts' hymns may be called 'Palladian'. This is a term borrowed from the history of architecture, and reasonably so, for architecture is the only one of the arts in which, for the English, the term 'baroque' can go unquestioned. The difference, in the English architecture of Watts' lifetime, between the baroque of Sir John Vanbrugh and the Palladianism of Lord Burlington, uncovers a tension within and beneath what literary history too indifferently and equably recognizes as 'Augustan'. If 'When I survey . . . ' is on its small scale a literary analogue to Vanbrugh's Castle Howard (1699–1726), more of Watts' hymns correspond to William Kent's Chiswick House for Burlington, built (c. 1725) to the specifications of Andrea Palladio in his *Quattro Libri dell' Architettura* (1570). The difference is between an art of calculated disproportion and even disjunction, and an art which eschews such devices as too sensational.

Without being fanciful, 'Palladian' is what we may call for instance a much less exciting yet estimable treatment of the Crucifixion in *Hymns and Spiritual Songs* I, 107:

Deceiv'd by subtle snares of hell,
Adam, our head, our father, fell!
When Satan, in the serpent hid,
Propos'd the fruit that God forbid.

Death was the threat'ning; death began
To take possession of the man;
His unborn race receiv'd the wound,
And heavy curses smote the ground.

But Satan found a worse reward;
Thus saith the vengeance of the Lord,
'Let everlasting hatred be
Betwixt the woman's Seed and thee.

The woman's Seed shall be my Son;
He shall destroy what thou hast done: –
Shall break thy head, and only feel
Thy malice raging at his heel.'

He spake – and bade four thousand years
Roll on; at length his Son appears:
Angels with joy descend to earth,
And sing the young Redeemer's birth.

Lo, by the sons of hell he dies;
But, as he hung 'twixt earth and skies,

He gave their prince a fatal blow,
And triumph'd o'er the powers below.

This is a narrative poem. And since in Palladian aesthetics proportion is
very nearly all in all, it is worth noting what the proportion is in Watts'
narrative between the Old Testament and the New. He gives four
stanzas to the Old Testament, two to the New. This is plainly at odds
with the account of Christian faith thrown out by a modern commentator: 'There's the high line, the religious line which goes from the birth of
Christ to the hypothetical return of that same Christ, with the time-
space in between these events seen as a vale of tears, a testing period.'[2]
Watts sees the birth of Christ not as the beginning of the Christian
narrative but as its culmination, in a real sense its end. Thus when the
modern commentator declares, 'This line is still a locus of belief, but no
longer a locus of live thought', we may agree with him, observing,
however, that the belief in question is certainly not Christian.

An incidental felicity in lines 15–16 of this poem is how Watts deals
with what seems incurably primitive in Genesis 3.15 where God,
cursing the serpent, ordains: 'And I will put enmitie between thee and
the woman, and between thy seed and her seed: it shall bruise thy head,
and thou shalt bruise his heele.' Watts' 'The malice raging at his heel'
elucidates, though not conclusively yet plausibly, what is meant by the
licence given to the serpent to 'bruise'. (A snake in the grass, a
venomous attack, a bruising encounter – primitive or not, the fable is
now sunk to a level in our language and imagination too deep to be
rooted out.) However, what makes this poem memorable is its last
quatrain. The fatal blow that the dying Christ gives to Satan is
metaphysical, obviously; and there is a metaphysical sense in which the
God-man in his death throes (though earlier also) is 'hung 'twixt earth
and skies'; but what vividly clinches the stanza and the whole poem is
that, as seen from ground level, the figure on the cross is physically a
hanging silhouette against the sky. That touch of physicality in what
has been a metaphysical drama strikes home very powerfully. But there
is nothing baroque about it. The touch comes just where a rationally
proportioned art would prescribe – as the climax, even (as in a good
joke) 'the pay-off'. And the atrociousness is nearer being acknowledged
in 'his dying crimson, like a robe' than in 'hung 'twixt earth and skies'.
(Certainly the first locution is the more decorative. But what it decor-
ates is, and is offered as, monstrous. English speakers have to learn from

[2] Kenneth White, 'Notes from an Outpost', *London Review of Books*, 6 July 1989.

Italian, Iberian and Latin-American art that 'decorative' need not mean 'unfeeling'.

Often Watts' Palladianism served him much less well. In another Crucifixion hymn, 'Infinite grief! amazing woe' (*Hymns and Spiritual Songs* II, 95), we read:

> Oh, the sharp pangs of smarting pain
>   My dear Redeemer bore,
> When knotty whips, and ragged thorns
>   His sacred body tore!
>
> But knotty whips and ragged thorns
>   In vain do I excuse,
> In vain I blame the Roman bands,
>   And the more spiteful Jews.
>
> 'Twere you, my sins, my cruel sins,
>   His chief tormentors were;
> Each of my crimes became a nail,
>   And unbelief the spear.

Leaving aside the prejudice against Jews (who are after all no sooner accused than they are exonerated), we surely and rightly feel rebellious at the all too elegant turn and return on 'knotty whips and ragged thorns'. It is not any allegiance to an anachronistic and in any case untenable aesthetic of 'immediacy' that makes us protest: 'Has he ever imagined what it is like to be whipped? And if what a whiplash does is called a smart, must there not be another word for what is painfully done by thorns bound round the temples?' The neatness of the return on 'knotty whips and ragged thorns' is bought at too steep a price. It is true that self-advertising elegance of this sort is valued differently in different ages; that Watts' age valued it probably too highly, as our period almost certainly rates it too low. But in any age there has to be a point at which order, harmony, composure are bought too dearly at the expense of fellow-feeling with torment and suffering. Watts, we may well think, too often did not accurately estimate the price that he was paying. 'When I survey the wondrous cross' represents one moment when he knew the price that was asked of him, and refused to pay it. By refusing that bargain he moved outside the orbit of contemporaries like John Byrom or Joseph Addison.

4

The 'Ending Up' of Isaac Watts

In 1736 Isaac Watts, a nonconformist minister then aged sixty-one, received a letter he could not have foreseen:

Poet, Divine, Saint, the delight, the guide the wonder of the virtuous world; permit, Reverend Sir, a stranger unknown, and likely to be for ever unknown, to desire one blessing from you in a private way. 'Tis this, that when you approach the Throne of Grace, and lift up holy hands, when you get closest to the Mercy-seat, and wrestle mightily for the peace of *Jerusalem*, you would breathe one petition for my soul's health. In return I promise you a share for life in my unworthy prayers, who honour you as a father and a brother (though differently ordered) and conclude myself,

Your affectionate humble Servant,
George Thomson

The effusiveness of this, its exalted tone, and the tropes which it so confidently deploys – 'the Throne of Grace', 'the Mercy-seat' – are virtually certain to set twentieth-century teeth on edge, whether those teeth are in a devout head or in the head of an unbeliever. Such floweriness, we have been schooled to think, must be insincere. And yet George Thomson, it is clear, neither requested nor expected to receive any benefit from this unsolicited tribute – apart from the solitary unworldly benefit that he asks for: 'one petition for my soul's health'. What is condemned by one generation as florid can seem to other generations no more than soberly exalted; and that consideration restricts very severely the practice of taking literary style as any register of 'sincerity'.

The date of this document unsettles other too commonly accepted notions. 'The Throne of Grace', 'the Mercy-seat' – these are tropes or (to take them at their most discredited) formulaic locutions that we associate with the evangelizing of the Wesleyan Revival. But in 1736 the Wesleyan movement was not yet off the ground. What the Wesley brothers revived was there to be revived; it was not altogether dead and sterile ground that they set out to fertilize. Methodist historiography has – inevitably, no doubt, and with the best intentions – consistently exaggerated the apathy and worldliness that the Wesleys contended with. It was not only inside the Wesley family that there persisted Christian devotion and saintliness through the two or three generations before John and Charles blew up an evangelical storm. Evangelicalism indeed, too often assumed to originate with the Wesley brothers, can be seen to be present and fermenting, in fact if not in name, before ever the brothers emerged on the stage of ecclesiastical history.

Moreover, this evangelicalism was already oecumenical. This is the significance of George Thomson's 'though differently ordered' – a parenthesis that comes clear when Thomson in a postscript identifies himself as 'Vicar of *St. Ginny's*, near *Camelford*, in *Cornwall*'. His tribute and plea to Isaac Watts come from a priest of the Established Church, to one whose Church was not established. The establishment of the Established Church mattered, to devout priests of that Church such as George Thomson, much less than many historians of our eighteenth century would have us believe. Thomson was looking for a spiritual father (a father-figure, so the dispiriting idiom of the present day would have it, and let that pass); if he found that figure in the priest of a Church less accredited than his own, he did not let that disconcert him. Such generosity, such blitheness, from both sides of the conformist/nonconformist divide, was common through many generations to nearly the end of the eighteenth century; and it is curious that historians of that century make so little of it.

And yet it is not so curious, after all. For it is notable how historians, even as they are chary of distinguishing Christians from non-Christians among the figures that they deal with from the century, distinguish very sharply among professing Christians between the conformists and the nonconformists. The latter, usually called 'dissenters', are thought to have existed in a sort of ghetto, partly state-imposed but more largely self-chosen, from which they infrequently but momentously erupted, brandishing republican banners. That there was never any such ghetto, or never one not infinitely porous, is what George Thomson's letter proves, along with similar documents from later decades. And such evidence as we have suggests that at any date, among nonconformists, monarchists far outnumbered republicans. But such charting of political allegiances is beside the point that for the present most interests me; which focusses rather on the way 'the nonconformist conscience' is still habitually appealed to, by commentators even on twentieth-

century England.[1] What are the peculiar characteristics of that conscience, distinguishing Watts' from George Thomson's, Philip Doddridge's from John Wesley's or William Cowper's, Orde Wingate's from
Cosmo Lang's? It seems that the question is never put – not by
present-day nonconformists who, disguised as Free Churchmen, maintain a profile so low as to be invisible; nor, less excusably, by present-
day Anglicans who seem content for the most part that 'conscience' be a
burden their nonconformist brethren shall carry for them. (On the
other hand, admit the confusing and comforting epithet 'social' – *social*
conscience' – and the Church of England will spring into action,
through commissions and committees naturally.)

Accordingly the Christian of whatever persuasion is reduced to
considering the context and overtones of rhetorical passages where that
phrase, 'the nonconformist conscience' is invoked. The most that can be
inferred from such passages is that the nonconformist conscience is
exacting, needling and insistent. But if these are not the characteristic
operations of the Christian conscience, then a lot of us have been
misreading the Pauline epistles; and if we have not thus misread, what
are the grounds for defining or in any way qualifying my, as it happens,
Anglican conscience as *nonconformist*?

George Thomson's letter to Watts was preserved by Thomas Gibbons in
his *Memoirs of the Rev. Isaac Watts D.D.* (1780). Gibbons' twelfth and last
chapter, where he prints letters received by Watts, is worth more than
all the preceding eleven. His attempt in some earlier pages to do justice
to Watts' poetry is well-intentioned but worthless; whereas some at least
of the questions to be asked about Watts as poet arise from a comparison
thrown out in passing by one of his correspondents. This was the
remarkable Frances, Countess of Hertford, in a letter written three
years after George Thomson's: 'I am truly sorry to find you complain of
any decay, but I am sure if you have any it must be bodily, and has no
other effect than that, which both Mr. Waller and *yourself* have so
happily described as *letting in light upon the soul*.' The diligent and helpful
Gibbons duly supplies the texts. Edmund Waller's lines are famous,
though not more famous than they deserve. They were designed, quite
deliberately it seems, to stand as Waller's farewell to the long and
illustrious but chequered career that ended with his death in 1687:

[1] See e.g. Robert Nye, 'The puritan, the savant and the clown', in *The Times*, 23 February
1991.

The soul's dark cottage batter'd and decay'd
Lets in new light through chinks that time has made;
Stronger by weakness, wiser men become,
As they draw near to their eternal home:
Leaving the old both worlds at once they view,
That stand upon the threshold of the new.

Watts' comparable poem was written in his youth, when Waller was not long dead. And so it may be supposed, though it might be hard to prove, that Watts had Waller's lines in mind as he wrote. In his *Horae Lyricae* (1706, revised 1709), Watts called his piece 'A sight of heaven in sickness':

Oft have I sat in secret sighs
    To feel my flesh decay,
Then groan'd aloud with frighted eyes
    To view the tottering clay;

But I forbid my sorrows now,
    Nor dares the flesh complain;
Diseases bring their profit too;
    The joy o'ercomes the pain.

My cheerful soul now all the day
    Sits waiting here and sings;
Looks through the ruins of her clay,
    And practises her wings.

Faith almost changes into sight,
    While from afar she spies
Her fair inheritance in light
    Above created skies.

Had but the prison-walls been strong,
    And firm without a flaw,
In darkness she had dwelt too long,
    And less of glory saw:

But now the everlasting hills
    Through ev'ry chink appear,
And something of the joy she feels,
    While she's a prisoner here.

The shines of heav'n rush sweetly in
    At all the gaping flaws;
Visions of endless bliss are seen,
    And native air she draws.

O may these walls stand tottering still,
   The breaches never close
If I must here in darkness dwell
   And all this glory lose!

Or rather let this flesh decay,
   The ruins wider grow
Till glad to see th' enlarged way
   I stretch my pinions too.

Asked to adjudicate between these stanzas and Waller's memorable
couplets, a modern reader might refuse the assignment. Waller's verses,
he might say, are too impassive, Watts' not impassive enough. What
circumscribes them both is a set of idioms and conventions – an earlier
criticism might have called the set 'neo-classical' – which he, a modern
post-Romantic, finds arbitrary and repugnant. A reader less sadly
incapacitated may decide without much fuss that none of Watts'
elaborations of the image of 'chinks' make up for the loss of Waller's
marmoreal succinctness. Watts' poem is only ragged 'prentice-work'.
But in lines like 'Faith almost changes into sight', or 'Diseases bring
their profit too', we see foreshadowed what was to be a distinctive
feature of the poet's maturity: a disconcerting Wordsworthian plainness
that rides recklessly over and into the pot-holes of bathos. Before it was
Wordsworthian, this diction was evangelical – in Charles Wesley, in
Cowper, and in the Watts who wrote hymns and versions of the Psalms.
Thus the Countess of Hertford's comparison was astute and can be
instructive. To be named in the same breath with Edmund Waller was
more than would be commonly allowed to Watts, by connoisseurs of
poetry, through the two centuries after Gibbons's *Memoirs*.

The topic is in any case a large one, perennial and intractable. What
does one say to a person whose life is drawing to its close, when that
person has consistently declared that life in time – his or anyone else's –
counts for nothing compared with the life laid up for him and them in
eternity?

   This is a different question from the one that confronts virtually all of
us, sooner or later: how to comfort the more or less loved one on his or
her death-bed. In those cases (not to be unfeeling about them) we may
be required to convey to the dying that the terror and uncertainty they
feel is understandable, and what we feel too; or else, if they die in hopes
of waking to eternity, we may feel up to assuring them that those hopes

are not unreasonable. But in the case of dying *saints* – for that, however embarrassingly, is what we seem to be concerned with – things are different: terror and uncertainty is what they have undertaken to save us from. That was in the contract; in the here and now we look to them, dying, to pay in full on all the promissory notes they have written in the past. We come near to throwing at them the proverb that Jesus cited (Luke 4.23): 'Physician, heal thyself.' The point is not simply that the death of a saint should be exemplary; if it is less than that, all his saintly witness is jeopardized. So it is that in all addresses to saints on their death-beds, there is unmistakably a note of menace: 'don't you dare not make an exemplary end!' He *must* die in an odour of sanctity. And so we look in vain for any evidence of how Watts himself experienced his protracted decline: if at any time the odour that assailed his nostrils was not that of sanctity and assurance, he was in honour bound not to reveal the fact. The debt of honour was binding; as he is reminded just under the surface of the most effusive protestations of reverence and gratitude. As against all the odds the always weakly Watts survived well into his seventies, the unspoken message sounds ever clearer: 'Don't fail us now!'

He was seventy-four when he got a letter from James Hervey (1714–58), author of *Meditations Among the Tombs* and in his day greatly admired as a luxuriant stylist:

Our excellent friend Dr. Doddridge informs me of the infirm condition of your health, for which reason I humbly beseech the Father of spirits, and the God of our life to renew your strength as the eagle's, and to recruit a lamp that has shone with distinguished lustre in his sanctuary; or, if this may not consist with the counsels of unerring wisdom, to make all your bed in your languishing, softly to untie the cords of animal existence, and enable your dislodging soul to pass triumphantly through the valley of death leaning on your beloved Jesus, and rejoicing in the greatness of his salvation.

Three years before Philip Doddridge himself had chanced his arm:

In the mean time, Sir, be assured that I am not a little animated in the various labours to which Providence has called me by reflecting that I have such a contemporary and especially such a friend, whose single presence would be to me as that of a cloud of witnesses here below to awaken my alacrity in the race which is set before me. And I am persuaded that, while I say this, I speak the sentiment of many of my brethren, even of various denominations; a consideration which I hope will do something towards reconciling a heart so generous as yours to a delay of that exceeding and eternal weight of glory which is now so nearly approaching. Yes, my honoured friend, you will I hope chearfully endure a little longer in life amidst all its infirmities from an assurance that, while God is pleased to maintain the exercise of your reason, it is hardly possible you should live in vain to the world or yourself. Every day, and every trial is brightening your crown, and rendering you still more and more meet for an inheritance among the saints in light. Every word which you drop from the pulpit has now surely its peculiar weight. The eyes of many are on their ascending prophet eagerly intent that they may catch if not his mantle, at least some divine sentence from his lips, which may long guide their ways, and warm their hearts. This solicitude your friends bring into those happy moments in which they are favoured with your converse in private, and, when you are retired from them, your prayers I doubt not largely contribute towards guarding your country, watering the church, and blessing the world. Long may they continue to answer these great ends!

Faced with a rhetoric so stately and fulsome as this which Hervey and Doddridge share, it is undeniably difficult to distinguish the sincere from the less sincere. The matter is complicated by the fact that Doddridge's sentences were meant for print, and appeared in print, as part of his dedication to Watts of his *The Rise and Progress of Religion in the Soul* (1744). The challenge, however, is thrown down. Whom shall we trust more – Hervey or Doddridge? After all, they say much the same things. Which of them means what they say? That is the question which literary criticism, at its most ambitious, undertakes to answer.

Among the impediments that confront us, though it may not show up at first glance, is the difficulty we all have about saints: our doubts about whether such human creatures ever existed, or can exist. The Roman Church, everyone knows, has its own elaborate machinery for identifying alleged saints, scrutinizing the claims made for them, on that basis dismissing many candidates and endorsing a few. The Protestant Churches, lacking such machinery and often vilifying it, unofficially recognize as saints only such persons as a majority of their peers have elevated to that rank. If enough people thought that Isaac Watts was a saint, then a saint was what he was. Thus 'saint', like any other title in a protestant polity, depends ultimately on popular suffrage and is perpetually open to challenge. It is only figuratively, or by analogy, that protestants can speak of saints – even though *The Book of Common Prayer* recognizes them as a class of historical persons, along with the more easily identified 'martyrs'. The sanctity of Watts – as of Doddridge also, for whom the same title has been claimed – has been, and is, challenged. And to those who have taken note of the challenge and found it persuasive, the tributes of George Thomson and the Countess of Hertford, of Hervey and Doddridge, cannot help but seem rhetorically excessive.

There could hardly be a clearer case of how critical judgement rests upon, and takes for granted, historical sympathy. Unless like Thomson or Frances Hertford we suppose the saint to be one who in the historical record really happens – we may define him in rapid shorthand as one who has not hopes of eternity, but an assurance of it – then of course any tribute addressed to him will seem vapid and excessive. Where we none the less discern such vapidity, as we surely may in the case of James Hervey, then we must seek the causes of it elsewhere than in Hervey's having wrong ideas about the religious life.

Thus one is led to think, not of course for the first time, that there is no scale for judging works of literature that is not undergirded (or else undermined) by valuations from outside literature altogether. Do we believe that saints are facts, or fictions? According as we opt for the first or the second alternative, our judgements of literature will differ – and by no means only of such a specialized genre as ecclesiastical biography. The bare possibility of sainthood, be it never so hypothetical, enhances our notions of what the human being is capable of, of the horizons inscribed for us. Accordingly, to dream of a study of literature that shall be 'value-free' is indeed a dream, and a sickly one. There is no way to judge the writings of and about Watts or Doddridge without reviewing how we feel about the Christian revelation.

5

The carnality of Charles Wesley

Wesley is a poet of vehement feeling. Coming upon him after reading Watts, what strikes us first is a steep rise in the emotional temperature assumed or exacted of us as readers (or as singers). This everyone notices, has always noticed – though the impression is allayed somewhat when we realise that not all the sacred poets in the generation before Wesley were so austere as Watts. The devout poetry of so unlikely a figure as Thomas Parnell, Pope's friend and comrade-in-arms, is for instance sometimes very fervent; and Watts' own friend, the once famous Elizabeth Rowe (whom Wesley can be shown to have studied), was a byword in her time for emotionalism that Watts indeed apologized for.

In any case, not feverish feeling so much as strong and muscular thought is what distinguishes such stanzas as these:

> Glory be to God on High,
>   And Peace on Earth descend;
> God comes down: He bows the Sky:
>   He shews himself our Friend!
> God th'Invisible *appears*,
>   God the Blest, the Great I AM
> Sojourns in this Vale of Tears,
>   And JESUS is his Name.
>
> Him the Angels all ador'd
>   Their Maker and their King:
> Tidings of their Humbled LORD
>   They now to Mortals bring:
> Emptied of his Majesty,
>   Of His dazzling Glories shorn,
> Being Source *begins to Be*,
>   And GOD himself is BORN!

Wesley's profligate use of italics and capitals and exclamation marks is

significant certainly, but it should not mislead us into thinking that
what we are offered is 'irrationality', or 'lazy and fanciful thought', or
'a perverse love of the paradoxical as such'.[1] On the contrary, it should
be clear that in a sentence like 'Being's Source begins to Be', our
intellectual faculties – not primarily the sympathies of the human heart,
but the energies of human Reason – are being stretched to the limit.
Surely such an expression represents the furthest that our Reason can
go in conceiving the unperceivable and the logically impossible. Wesley
was a creature of 'the Age of Reason'; and the date when these verses
were composed (c. 1745) is entirely appropriate. As has been said,
'once we have seized the point that in the Enlightenment the poetic
imagination could and did quite naturally proceed by way of *abstraction*,
we perceive that it could hardly stop short of those awesomely abstract
because paradoxical concepts that are the matter of theology'.[2]

The issue takes on new interest when we return these stanzas to the
context in which they first appeared. That context was re-established
by Frank Baker in his invaluable and too little esteemed *Representative
Verse of Charles Wesley* (1962). The context was a pamphlet of eighteen
poems under the title *Hymns for the Nativity of our Lord*. Published in 1745
without author's name, printer's name or date, it went through at least
twenty editions in the poet's lifetime. It is particularly notable because,
as Frank Baker establishes, it seems to afford evidence of how John
Wesley privately regarded his brother's poetry, and so of how their
poetic tastes differed. John declared 'the very best hymn in the collection' to be the eighteenth and last:

> All Glory to GOD in the Sky,
>   And Peace upon Earth be restor'd!
> O JESUS, exalted on high,
>   Appear our omnipotent Lord:
> Who meanly in *Bethlehem* born,
>   Didst stoop to redeem a lost Race,
> Once more to thy Creatures return
>   And reign in thy Kingdom of Grace.
>
> When Thou in our Flesh didst appear,
>   All Nature acknowledg'd thy Birth;
> Arose the acceptable Year,
>   And Heaven was open'd on Earth;
> Receiving its Lord from above,

---

[1] See Karl Barth, *Evangelical Theology. An Introduction* (Edinburgh, 1963), p. 92.
[2] Donald Davie, *Dissentient Voice. Enlightenment & Christian Dissent* (Notre Dame, 1982), p. 20.

The World was *united* to bless
The Giver of Concord and Love,
    The Prince and the Author of Peace.

O wouldst Thou again be made known,
    Again in thy Spirit descend,
And set up in each of thine own
    A Kingdom that never shall end!
Thou only art able to bless,
    And make the glad Nations obey,
And bid the dire Enmity cease,
    And bow the whole World to thy Sway.

Come then to thy Servants again,
    Who long thy Appearing to know,
Thy quiet and peaceable Reign
    In Mercy establish below:
All Sorrow before Thee shall fly,
    And Anger and Hatred be o'er,
And Envy and Malice shall die,
    And Discord afflict us no more.

No horrid Alarum of War
    Shall break our Eternal Repose;
No sound of the Trumpet is there,
    Where JESUS'S Spirit o'erflows;
Appeased by the Charms of thy Grace
    We all shall in Amity join,
And kindly each other embrace,
    And love with a Passion like Thine.

This is stately and decorous, and might even be called majestic, were it not for the tripping anapaestic metre. Seldom in celebrations of Christ as Prince of Peace is the peace that He brings conceived in such public and political terms as here by Wesley – not for nothing did the poem appear in the year of a Jacobite rebellion. What it has no hint of is paradox: 'meanly' ('meanly in Bethlehem born') is as near as it chooses to come to 'Beings Source *begins to Be*, / And GOD himself is BORN!'

It was not paradox, however, that John Wesley singled out as unacceptable in other hymns of the sequence; it was something he called 'namby-pambical'. 'Namby-pamby', a derisive play on the name of Ambrose Philips, whose pastorals Pope had famously savaged in *The Guardian*, points to a kind or feature of poetic diction that has never been satisfactorily defined except as 'baby-talk'. And that seems to be

all that it meant for John Wesley. For number six in the sequence
(Baker, No. 40) seems to be one that he disliked as 'namby-pambical',
and his own copy was marked so as to require that the third, fourth and
fifth stanzas be omitted:

> Go see the King of Glory,
> Discern the Heavenly Stranger,
>   So poor and mean,
>   His Court an Inn,
> His Cradle is a Manger:
> Who from his Father's Bosom
> But now for Us Descended,
>   Who built the Skies,
>   On Earth he lies,
> With only Beasts attended.
>
> Whom all the Angels worship,
> Lies hid in Human Nature;
>   Incarnate see
>   The Deity,
> The Infinite Creator!
> See the Stupendous Blessing
> Which GOD to us hath given!
>   A Child of Man,
>   In Length a Span,
> Who fills both Earth and Heaven.
>
> Gaze on that Helpless Object
> Of endless Adoration!
>   Those Infant-Hands
>   Shall burst our Bands,
> And work out our Salvation;
> Strangle the crooked Serpent,
> Destroy his Works for ever,
>   And open set
>   The Heavenly Gate
> To every True Believer.

There is plenty of paradox here, and its presence is what stops the verses
from being mawkish (which is presumably what John needlessly feared
when thinking them 'namby-pambical'). It seems to have been the
literalness of the Holy Babe that offended him: 'In Length a Span . . .',
'that Helpless Object . . .' Yet in both these cases Wesley uses the
line-ending in a way to vindicate a strophic structure that might

otherwise seem merely *tricksy*. The creature 'in Length a Span' turns out
to have *spanned* 'both Earth and Heaven'; and the helpless object of
adults' care and ministrations turns out to be the 'object' (in another
sense) 'of endless Adoration'. As the verse-line turns, so the 'turning
out' is enacted; yet the first sense is not cancelled out by the second – the
child remains a helpless 'object' (full stop), even after he has been
revealed as the object *of* something else (adoration). These are ambiguities – more properly double-meanings – such as the most sophisticated
verse-writers might be proud to contrive. Moreover if, as seems likely,
John Wesley was alarmed by the physicality in these renderings of the
Christ-child, he was in for a worse disturbance when, in number sixteen
of the sequence (Baker, No. 50), his brother required him to recognize
that God Incarnate sucked at a human nipple:

> Our God ever blest
> With Oxen doth rest,
> Is nurst by his Creature and hangs at the Breast.

We may suspect that John Wesley, who fathered no children, was
never at ease with or about babies, their messiness, their demanding-
ness. If this distaste or discomfort extended to sexuality in general, of
which babies are a symptom and sometimes a consequence, there is
evidence in his life as well as his writings that this was indeed one area
in which he differed from, and fell short of, his brother the poet.
Southey delicately skirted this area when he compared the brothers:

But even if John Wesley's marriage had proved as happy in all other respects as
Charles's, it would not have produced upon him the same sedative effect.
Entirely as these two brothers agreed in opinions and principles, and cordially
as they had acted together during so many years, there was a radical difference
in their disposition. Of Charles it has been said, by those who knew him best,
that if ever there was a human being who disliked power, avoided pre-
eminence, and shrunk from praise, it was he: whereas no conqueror or poet was
ever more ambitious than John Wesley. Charles could forgive an injury; but
never again trusted one whom he had found treacherous. John could take men
a second time to his confidence, after the greatest wrongs and the basest usage:
perhaps, because he had not so keen an insight into the characters of men as his
brother; perhaps, because he regarded them as his instruments, and thought
that all other considerations must give way to the interests of the spiritual
dominion which he had acquired.[3]

---

[3] *The Life of Wesley, and Rise & Progress of Methodism*, 3rd edn by Charles Culbert Southey,
  including notes by S. T. Coleridge, vol. 2, 186–7.

There may in this be something partisan; what needs to be added in any case is that – as anecdotes preserved by Southey attest – Charles was, in emergencies, as intrepid and resolute as John.

Charles' intellectualism is as evident in 'hangs at the Breast' as in 'Being's Source begins to Be'. The first observation is a necessary corollary of the second. For God to become a human baby meant that he had to take on all the features of human babyhood: the Creator became one of His creatures, and thereby took on all the conditions (helplessness, need to be fed, perhaps squalling, certainly toilet-training) that constrain the creaturely. The poet could see and argue this through as his brother, the preacher, did not or could not or chose not to; though it is hard to see, when one thinks about it, what else Incarnation is all about. When we sing 'Away in a Manger' and declare 'No crying He makes', we have so far as I can see no scriptural or other authority for this assertion, and we are being mawkish where Charles Wesley was not. The same invaluable literal-mindedness that took Christ's promise of peace to mean that the Pretender's army would halt at Preston if not before, perceives also that the infant God–man would suck, perhaps hungrily, at the teat.

Many years ago Martha Winburn England decided that Wesley was ineradicably a vulgar writer.[4] Being so literal-minded, he could not help but seem so, to others besides his brother. But that is to fudge the issue. What Ms England put her finger on was not a seeming but a fact. Wesley *is* vulgar, not in any sense that can be wheedlingly glossed as 'demotic' or 'democratic'; quite simply, his feel for the English language was anything but fastidious:

> Why then, Thou Universal Love,
>   Should any of thy Grace despair?
> To All, to All, Thy bowels move,
>   But straitned in our own we are.

A correspondent who has forgotten more about Wesley than I have ever known[5] has pointed out to me that of course for this use of 'bowels' to mean (*OED*) 'the seat of the tender and sympathetic emotions', Wesley has ample precedents in the Authorized Version. The *Dictionary* cites usages from other English texts as early as the fourteenth century and as late as the nineteenth. My correspondent helpfully points out the

---

[4] Martha Winburn England and John Sparrow, *Hymns Unbidden* (New York, 1966).
[5] Professor James Dale of McMaster University.

particular text that Wesley doubtless had in mind. It is 2 Corinthians
6.11–12:

> O yee Corinthians, our mouth is open unto you, our heart is enlarged.
> Yee are not straitned in us, but yee are straitned in your owne bowels.

But though my friend is doubtless right, this hardly disposes of my
discomfort. For if King James' translator may be trusted, the emotional
constriction with which Paul affectionately reproaches the Corinthians
is contrasted to a movement not in his bowels but in, perhaps sig-
nificantly, his *heart*. It is Wesley, not Paul, who compares bowels with
bowels. And it is Wesley who, raising the stakes from the Apostle to his
Lord, has to assert that the latter's bowels 'move' not just to a Cor-
inthian congregation but 'To All, to All'. Accordingly it is from Wesley,
not from Paul, that we get the impression that, whereas 'straitness' or
constriction in the bowels is a bad thing, looseness of the bowels is good.

If with Martha England we find such a usage 'vulgar', we must not be
misunderstood. Certainly we cannot think, as some of our grandparents
did, that any reference to bowel-movements, outside of strictly medical
contexts, is a vulgarity. The lack of fastidiousness is not in the carnal
matters that Wesley readily refers to – on the contrary, as we seemed to
find in his treatment of babies, that is one of his strengths which is hard
to parallel; the lack of fastidiousness that we may reprehend lies in his
art, in the lack of control over his artistic medium, his language, which
traps him into seeming to say things that he did not intend.

Martha England proposed that vulgarity of this kind was something
that Wesley shared with William Blake; though it would surely be hard
to find in Blake anything so off-putting and heedless as these verses from
Wesley in 1741. Yet she was surely right to regard such *detritus* as the
unavoidable spilling over of a genius that is, as Wesley's was and Blake's
also, prophetic and volcanic. Wesley is – like perhaps Walt Whitman – a
poet from whom the abundant dross has to be tolerated for the sake of
the not infrequent gold. His prodigious fertility suggests as much.

This means that Wesley, again like Whitman, is a master whom later
poets learn from at their peril. Derek Walcott, recalling his childhood
on a Caribbean island, is doubtless representative of many who learned
from Wesley how English could go into poetry:

> Once, past a wooden vestry,
> down still, colonial streets,
> the lifted hymns of Wesley
> were cords of miners' throats;

> Their faith was calm as timber,
> as unadorned as wood,
> their truth, as I remember,
> more sensed than understood;
>
> In treachery or in union
> despite an Empire's wrong,
> I made my first communion
> there, with the English tongue.[6]

But Wesley's language is not, in Spenser's words about Chaucer, a 'well of English pure and undefiled'; nor is it – despite Walcott's 'timber' and 'wood' – the idiom of carpenters and joiners, sturdy artisans. It is always in danger of being streaked and sullied by lapses into sectarian cant which sometimes, as in the verses about 'bowels', seem to depend on a sort of physicality that we may call morbid. E. P. Thompson, in his *Making of the English Working Class* (1964), was right to detect this element in the Wesleyan hymns, though he built on it outrageously so as to convict the Wesleyan Movement generally.[7] It may seem to derive from the lingering attachment to the hymn-idioms of the Moravian Brethren of Count Zinzendorf, whose evangelizing in America first spurred the youthful Wesley brothers to emulation. That was the supposition of the nineteenth-century hymnist Josiah Conder, writing to his son in 1838. Conder, after quoting reverently from one of Wesley's hymns, explains:

I did not insert the hymn in our collection, because it is unsuitable for congregational use; and like many other beautiful hymns of almost impassioned devotion, by the same author, it savours too much of the mystic school of piety, which is not the *Pauline*. There is nothing monastic, feminine, or mawkish, in the fervent devotion of the Apostle to his Master and Lord. The atmosphere he lived in was not that of a cave or a cell, and yet it was intense, and carried him through martyrdom. Now the devotion of the Romish mystic, from which that of Wesley and Zinzendorf was borrowed as regards its style, is not of this masculine fibre, of this daylight character. In turning from the inspired writings of Paul and John to such hymns and devotional writings, you feel that you are passing into another region and temperature. At the same time, when one is cold, and cannot have sunshine, artificial warmth may be both pleasant and salutary; and a devout person may envy the feelings which inspired many of these compositions, with all their defects, and catch from them a genial glow.[8]

[6] Derek Walcott, from 'Eulogy to W. H. Auden', *The New Republic*, 21 November 1983.
[7] See Donald Davie, *A Gathered Church* (1978), pp. 45–7.
[8] Eustace R. Conder, *Josiah Conder. A Memoir* (1857), p. 282.

The nervous overemphasis here on manliness and the open air smacks of Victorian muscular Christianity, but it detects accurately enough something in Wesley's poetry which, though it may not impugn the quality of his devotion, certainly places his verse-style somewhere off-centre. On the other hand 'influence' can never adequately explain such a phenomenon, if only because influence can never be exerted on any one not temperamentally or otherwise ready for it.

In any case, once more we have to recognize that Wesley's 'vulgarity' manifests itself not as fervently unfocussed feeling, but as crabbed and congested *thought*. In his earlier hymns, which proclaim their Moravian heritage by using mixed metre (for instance, iambic trimeters mixed with trochaic tetrameters), there is confusion of the first person singular with the second, and this produces the oddity that the Deity, addressed in the second person, can be subjected to hectoring commands:

> See the Travail of thy Soul,
>   Saviour, and be satisfy'd.

Yet this is not simple sloppiness, but comes about by a tortuous logic. For since at the moment of Conversion in the Wesleyan scheme of things the devotee exclaims, 'My soul henceforth be thine, O Lord', it follows that that soul can thereafter be described as 'His', or, in direct address, 'thine'. This happens in 'O Filial Diety' (1739; Baker, No. 3):

> O Filial Deity,
>   Accept my New-born Cry!
> See the Travail of thy Soul,
>   Saviour, and be satisfy'd;
> Take now, possess me whole,
>   Who for Me, for Me hast dy'd!
>
> Of Life thou art the Tree,
>   My Immortality!
> Feed this tender Branch of thine,
>   Ceaseless Influence derive,
> Thou the true, the heav'nly Vine,
>   Grafted into Thee I live.
>
> Of Life the Fountain Thou,
>   I know – I feel it Now!
> Faint and dead no more I droop:
>   Thou art in me: Thy Supplies
> Ev'ry Moment springing up
>   Into Life Eternal rise.

Thou the Good Shepherd art,
From Thee I n'er shall part:
Thou my Keeper and my Guide,
Make me still thy Tender Care,
Gently lead me by thy Side,
Sweetly in thy Bosom bear.

Thou art my Daily Bread;
O CHRIST, thou art my Head:
Motion, Virtue, Strength to Me,
Me thy Living Member flow;
Nourish'd I, and fed by Thee,
Up to Thee in all things grow.

Prophet, to me reveal
Thy Father's perfect Will.
Never Mortal spake like Thee,
Human Prophet like Divine;
Loud and strong their Voices be,
Small and still and inward Thine!

On Thee my Priest I call;
Thy Blood aton'd for all.
Still the Lamb as slain appears;
Still Thou stand'st before the Throne,
Ever off'ring up thy Pray'rs,
These presenting with thy own.

JESU! Thou art my King,
From Thee my Strength I bring!
Shadow'd by thy mighty Hand,
Saviour, who shall pluck me thence?
Faith supports, by Faith I stand
Strong as thy Omnipotence.

O Filial Deity,
Accept my New-born Cry!
See the Travail of thy Soul,
Saviour, and be satisfy'd;
Take me now, possess me whole,
Who for Me, for Me hast dy'd!

(The muddling of first with second person disconcerted Wesleyans
quite early on: as early as 1782 the penultimate line of the seventh
stanza was changed to read 'my prayers', but the original reading must
be right, to make sense of the italicized 'These' in the next line.)

Wesley wants to break down distinctions: principally, the distinction between the devotee and his Saviour; secondly, and consequentially, the distinction between one devotee and the next. If this involves eradicating the distinction between first and second persons singular, that is a violence to language which he is willing to perpetrate. His earnestness – more precisely, his ruthlessness – shows in the way he rehearses the scriptural metaphors for the union of the devotee with God, moving from the acceptable analogies with viniculture and grafting, through the unexceptional icon of the Good Shepherd cradling the lost sheep, to (in his fifth stanza) the far more dangerous and dubious trope of 'members'.

'Church-members', 'committee-members' – these common and insipid modern usages are hard to square with what the Old Testament makes of 'members': with Job saying (17.7), 'Mine eye also is dimme by reason of sorrow, and all my members are as a shadow'; or with the Psalmist saying (Psalm 139), 'Thine eyes did see my substance yet being imperfect, and in thy booke all my members were written, which in continuation were fashioned . . .' These usages, which are echoed more than once in the Pauline epistles, have more to do with the once common euphemism that called the penis 'the virile member' than with the modern implications of 'committee-man'. And they cast an unavoidable oblique light on such treasured and consoling texts as Ephesians 4.25: 'Wherefore put away lying, speake every man truth with his neighbour; for we are members one of another'; or, in the next chapter of Ephesians (5.29–30),

> For no man ever yet hated his own flesh; but nourisheth and cherisheth it, even as the Lord the church:
> For we are members of his body, of his flesh, and of his bones.

Charles Wesley is true to his churchmanship, always stricter and more vehement than his brother's, by starting his stanza about 'Me thy Living Member' with 'Thou art my Daily Bread', recalling what is said when the wafer is offered in the Anglican Eucharist: 'The body of Christ'. Wesley took in all seriousness his own perception that 'Whom all the Angels worship / Lies hid in Human Nature'. God's incarnation means that He is present in our carnality, in all our members, including the most carnal. The poet in declaring this has not departed from tradition; he has merely pushed the tradition to its unavoidable limit. And the insistent physicality of his images and allusions has in such a case nothing morbid; it merely follows out the implications of what is an article of belief.

Wesley's 'Hymn for Easter-Day' is 'Christ the Lord is ris'n today', which of course is still widely sung by all denominations, though drastically truncated and tricked out with 'Hallelujahs'. Not now sung are stanzas 8, 9 and 10:

> Scarce on Earth a Thought bestow.
> Dead to all we leave below,
> Heav'n our Aim, and lov'd Abode,
> Hid our Life with CHRIST in GOD!
>
> Hid; till CHRIST our Life appear,
> Glorious in his Members here:
> Join'd to Him, we then shall shine
> All Immortal, all Divine!
>
> Hail the Lord of Earth and Heav'n!
> Praise to Thee by both be giv'n:
> Thee we greet Triumphant now;
> Hail the Resurrection Thou!

'Resurrection Thou' (rather than 'Resurrected Thee') introduces again the ambiguity involved when Jesus is addressed in the second person; grammatically, though surely in no other way, the concluding 'Thou' could even be a vocative. And whereas we do not think that 'Glorious in his Members here' means that Christ is physically *dismembered*, that is not a possibility we can easily exclude. Semantically and etymologically 'member' and 'dismember' lie so close together that the one implies the possibility of the other. This is a fact of language, that neither Wesley as writer nor we as readers can get away from.

Body, Head, Members, Constitution – these are dead metaphors which we apply to many secular associations as well as to the associations we call churches, thinking (if we think of the matter at all) that we are dealing only in formal analogies. Wesley is determined to breathe new life into them, whatever the disconcerting implications. However, he is not always consistent:

> Appear with Clouds on *Sion*'s Hill,
> Thy Word and Mystery to fulfil,
>   Thy Confessors t'approve,
> Thy Members on thy Throne to place,
> And stamp thy Name on every Face
>   In glorious heavenly Love.

In all the range of scriptural meanings for 'members', from the Book of

Job to the Epistle to the Ephesians, there is none that can make sense here, except ludicrously. The poem where this stanza appears is apocalyptic, appearing as it did among seventeen *Hymns for the Year 1756*, a year widely thought to herald the apocalypse, marked as it was by pestilence, famine and the outbreak of war, as well as by earthquake a few months before in Lisbon. And of apocalyptic writings, notably the Book of Revelation which is plainly in Wesley's mind at this point, it is sometimes said that we should not look for imagery that is poetically coherent. Apocalyptic texts, it is sometimes contended, transcend such considerations. It is safer to say, so long as poetry is our concern, that such texts fail to satisfy. And in such a case we have not just poetic vulgarity, but incoherence; religiose *cant* does not merely tarnish these texts, considered as poems, it destroys them. And this happens with Wesley more often than his admirers are ready to acknowledge.

But of course to admit this is by no means to fall in with the common unthinking assumption that the Wesley hymns are, as poems, not worth bothering with. Charles Wesley sounds notes that are outside the range, or outside the intentions, of any other sacred poet in English. I have found myself stressing one such note: what I have called, perhaps provokingly, his *carnality*. But as we have seen, this is only a special case of his literal-mindedness. Yet to call this, as I have, 'invaluable' is surely very odd praise to give to a poet. For from poets we have been led to expect, above all, inventive and illuminating metaphors, and metaphor is what the literal mind has trouble with. Does it make sense to say that the act of metaphor was foreign to Wesley's cast of mind? At first blush this seems ridiculous: Wesley's verse is full of metaphors, it is highly figurative. However, the metaphors seem to get into his language in two ways: in the first place, because he was very solidly grounded in Latin, he is splendidly aware of the metaphors hidden in latinate words, the physicality that etymology uncovers in them when they seem most abstract;[9] and secondly, because Wesley's language is insistently scriptural, it abounds in metaphors taken from the Bible. Yet as we have seen with 'bowels' and 'members', Wesley seems not always to recognize that, when he leans on Scripture, metaphor is what he is dealing with. The physicality inherent in 'bowel' and 'member' is what he does not heed, and sometimes his heedlessness trips him up. The literalism

---

[9] See 'The Classicism of Charles Wesley', in Donald Davie, *Purity of Diction in English Verse* (1952).

that in many happier cases welcomes physicality, in these cases excludes it, or (rather) entertains it unawares. This makes Wesley a very strange poet indeed; one that later poets, among them hymn-writers, were ill-advised to emulate.

6

Psalmody as translation

In *The Oxford Companion to Music* we are told of 'psalmody': 'By this term is generally meant the study of the tunes for metrical versions of the psalms and for hymns, but it can, obviously, have a wider range of meaning.' Since we are concerned not in the least with tunes but with *wording*, the meaning we give to 'psalmody' must lie within the wider range that Percy Scholes allows for. Our authority may be Isaac Watts as cited in the *Oxford English Dictionary*: 'We are to suit part of our psalmody to the gospel-state as well as borrow part from the Old Testament.' For here, whatever we may think of Watts' categorical injunction, it is plain that he takes 'psalmody' to denote a literary, not a musical, genre.

In that sense, psalmody is clearly a special case within verse-translation generally. And translation has lately come in for a great deal of theoretical attention – much of that attention, notably the much-lauded Walter Benjamin's, at too high a level of abstraction to be immediately useful to translators or to their readers. In any case it is noticeable that when the theorists stoop to consider cases, they seldom examine translations of the Psalms, whether directly from the Hebrew or from the Vulgate. And yet very often their conclusions vindicate eighteenth-century psalmodists like Watts and Christopher Smart. Consider only Watts' declaration above that the psalmodist must suit his versions 'to the gospel-state', as well as to the Old Testament. Whereas older notions of translation, such as H. Leigh Bennett's in Julian's *Dictionary of Hymnology*, ruled out such liberties as plainly licentious, more recent discussions have tended to agree that such anachronistic modernizing, whether covert or declared, is inseparable from translation considered as an imaginative endeavour. Ezra Pound's *Homage to Sextus Propertius* (1917), where Pound made the ancient Roman elegist allude to both Wordsworth and Yeats, has been taken as the modern work that forced this recognition on English-speaking readers.[1] From this standpoint, when Watts and following him Smart explicitly declare themselves Christian translators of a pre-Christian text, they are commendably making overt what must have been the case (though mostly unacknowledged) for psalmodists before them, and after them to the present day. It thus becomes possible, indeed imperative, to consider their versions of the Psalms as translations, rather than huddling them away under some apologetic label like 'adaptation' or 'paraphrase'.

It may be thought that these psalm-versions are a special case in so far as they were intended not to be read but sung, and sung in congregations. This is almost certainly wrong. I have seen no evidence that Smart's versions were, any of them, ever congregational; and those by Watts that were adopted for congregational worship could be put to that use only after drastic abbreviations and changes, transforming them from psalms strictly considered into hymns. Whereas most English versions of the Psalter, or any part of it, seem to have been composed with at least a wistful hope that a congregation might some time render them in unison, by saying if not by chanting or singing, yet some of the most splendid were clearly made with no such purpose in mind. Probably the most splendid of all is the Sidney Psalter, for the most part and at its best the work not of Philip Sidney but his sister. Rather plainly the Countess of Pembroke, who never printed her versions, must have meant them to minister only to private, not public devotions. In other words, they were meant to be read. And Watts and Smart also must have had in mind readers, far more than congregational singers.

It is quite otherwise, to be sure, with the so-called Old Version (by Sternhold and Hopkins, 1551) and New Version (by Tate and Brady, 1698). Both these psalters, the first approved by Edward VI, the second by William III, were intended for congregational use, and were used through many decades by most Anglican congregations throughout the kingdom. For students of the eighteenth century Tate's and Brady's Psalter ought therefore to be unavoidable, and yet it is routinely avoided. The most respectable reason for this is the unaccountably bad press that Nahum Tate has had, from his own day to ours.[2] The *Dictionary of National Biography* declares him roundly 'poetaster'. He was

---

[1] See e.g. Daniel M. Hooley, *The Classics in Paraphrase* (1988). We may acknowledge that Pound's poem established a precedent for modern translators without entering on the vexed question whether it is itself a translation.

[2] Though Nicholas Brady, who outlived his collaborator, was himself a poet, and though no one knows how he and Tate shared out their labours, there is a conspiratorial consensus down the centuries to blame Tate for whatever is wrong in their version.

sneered at in print by both Pope and Thomas Parnell, though in neither case very mordantly. No one since Walter Scott seems to have pondered why Dryden patronized him and collaborated with him. If we recognize Tate (1652–1715) as the author of 'While shepherds watched their flocks by night', we may well wonder if he has been given his due; and the suspicion grows stronger when we note that his version of the 34th Psalm survives into most of our hymn-books as 'Through all the changing scenes of life'.

Madeleine Forell Marshall and Janet Todd have usefully compared the Old and the New Version in respect of Psalm 102, or of its first half. They comment that the changes which Tate and Brady made to Sternhold's version 'to modern ears, seem to introduce a language and a religious experience that is less immediate. The subjectivity masks a failure in the communication between the singer and the Lord, and the singer is more inclined to turn inward, to contemplate his own feelings.'[3] We may wonder whether 'modern ears' are so averse to introspection as Marshall and Todd suppose; still they are surely right to imply that in both psalms and hymns a very little 'subjectivity' goes quite far enough. Both genres are essentially *public*; and even though Watts and Smart must have known that their psalms would be read mostly by solitary individuals in private, they observed decorum so as to write *as if* for public, communal occasions. Potentially more damaging is Marshall's and Todd's observation that the New Version is conspicuously less concise than the Old. In what follows the proportion is eighteen lines (Old Version) to twenty-four (New):

(For as the smoke doth fade, so doo my dayes consume and fall.)	Each cloudy Portion of my life Like scatter'd Smoak expires;
And as a herth, my bones are burnt: my hart is smitten dead,	My shriv'led Bones are like a Hearth That's parch'd with constant Fires.
And withers as the grass, that I forget to eate my bread.	
By reason of my groning voyce, My bones cleave to my skinne:	My heart, like Grass that feels the Blast Of some infectious Wind, Is Wither'd so with Grief, that scarce My needful Food I mind.
As pelicane of wilderness, such case now am I in.	
And as an oule in desart is, loe I am such a one:	By reason of my sad Estate I spend my Breath in Groans; My Flesh is worn away, my Skin Scarce hides my starting Bones.

[3] Madeleine Forell Marshall and Janet Todd, *English Congregational Hymns in the Eighteenth Century* (Lexington, Kentucky, 1982), p. 17.

I watch, and as a sparrow on
   the house top am alone.
Loe dayly in reprocheful wise,
   mine enmies doo me scorne
And they that doo against me rage,
   Against me they have sworne.

I'm like a Pelican become,
   That does in Desarts mourn;
Or like an Owl that sits all day
   On barren Trees forlorn.

In Watchings or in restless Dreams
   I spend the tedious Night;
Like Sparrows, that on Houses tops
   To sit alone delight.

All day by railing Foes I'm made
   The object of their Scorn;
Who all, inspir'd with furious Rage,
   Have my Destruction sworn.

Though the Old Version is so much shorter than the New, it can hardly be thought more economical. Writing that will not use the comparison 'as' without adding 'such case now am I in', or 'loe I am such a one', can hardly be considered terse. But a weightier objection is that what Sternhold and Hopkins are writing is not in fact verse. Not poetry; that is out of the question. But verse (from *versus*, a turn) is necessarily defined by what happens at verse-endings, at the turn from one verse-line into the next; and it is evident that at the end of the first line above, of the fifth and of the thirteenth (none of them rhyming, incidentally), no expressive use of the turn is made or even sought for. To be sure, Sternhold and Hopkins probably conceived they were writing fourteen-ers. At all these points the notional or real pause that the line-ending enforces is a mere hindrance, a gulp. That the Old Version should have held its own through so many generations (though always reviled by some readers) ought to dispel any illusions we may have about the level of poetic taste and understanding in the literate Elizabethan and Caroline populace. By contrast Tate and Brady are at all events writing *verse*; they respect the integrity of the verse-line, so that when they make an enjambement ('My Flesh is worn away, my Skin/Scarce hides ... ') we register this as a welcome variation; we look for (and find) an expressive intention and effect. After Tate and Brady no English psalmodist, however pious or evangelizing his chief intention, could think that what he was engaged on was anything but an art. Historic-ally this was momentous; and for bringing it about, Tate and Brady deserve more credit than is commonly allowed to them.

    In Julian's *Dictionary*, H. Leigh Bennett, to whom Julian entrusted the article on English psalters, delivered himself of an astonishing judgement about Isaac Watts' psalter of 1719, *Psalms of David Imitated in the Language of the New Testament*. 'Taken as a whole', he says, 'it is not better than Tate and Brady. There is a want of restraining reverence about it; and the turgid epithets, and gaudy ornament dishonour the simple grandeur of the original.' Watts would have been dumbfounded, for gaudy ornament and indeed any ornament except the most modest was precisely what he thought he had eschewed. And modern readers like Harry Escott and John Hoyles agree with him, crediting him with what Escott calls 'artistic kenosis': 'Watts had to lay his poetic glories aside, and dress the profound message of the gospel in homespun verse and the language of the people.'[4] Even those like Pope who thought Watts' 'art of sinking' a perverse and ludicrous enterprise, had no doubt that his endeavour, ill-judged or not, was such as he declared it to be. The truth is surely that H. Leigh Bennett's generation had become so deaf to the whole linguistic and rhetorical register of English Augustan verse that they could not hear differences within that register, as for instance between Pope's Homer and his Epistles. It is a condition that afflicts some unfortunates still.

To match Watts fairly against Tate and Brady, we may take as our specimen Psalm 74:

Tate and Brady	Watts
Why has thou cast us off, O God?	Will God for ever cast us off?
Wilt thou no more return?	His wrath for ever smoke –
O why against thy chosen flock	Against the people of his love,
Does thy fierce anger burn?	His little chosen flock?
Think on thy ancient purchase, Lord,	Think of the tribes, so dearly bought
The land that is thy own;	With their Redeemer's blood;
By thee redeem'd, and Sion's mount,	Nor let thy Zion be forgot,
Where once thy glory shone.	Where once thy glory stood.
O come, and view our ruin'd state!	Lift up thy feet, and march in haste;
How long our troubles last!	Aloud our ruin calls;
See how the foe, with wicked rage,	See what a wide, and fearful waste
Has laid thy temple waste!	Is made within thy walls.
Thy foes blaspheme thy name where late	Where once thy churches pray'd and sang
Thy zealous servants pray'd;	Thy foes profanely roar:
The heathen there, with haughty pomp,	Over thy gates their ensigns hang,
Their banners have display'd.	Sad tokens of their power.

[4] Harry Escott, *Isaac Watts Hymnographer* (1962), p. 26; quoted and endorsed by Hoyles, *The Waning of the Renaissance 1640–1740* (1971), p. 240.

Those curious carvings, which did once
   Advance the artist's fame,
With ax and hammer they destroy
   Like works of vulgar frame.

Thy holy temple they have burnt;
   And what escap'd the flame
Has been profan'd, and quite defac'd,
   Though sacred to thy name.

Thy worship wholly to destroy
   Maliciously they aim'd;
And all the sacred places burnt,
   Where we thy praise proclaim'd.

Yet of thy presence thou vouchsaf'st
   No tender signs to send;
We have no prophet now, that knows
   When this sad state shall end.

How are the seats of worship broke!
   They tear thy buildings down;
And he who deals the heaviest stroke
   Procures the chief renown.

With flames they threaten to destroy
   Thy children in their nest;
'Come, let us burn at once!' they cry,
   'The temple and the priest.'

And still, to heighten our distress,
   Thy presence is withdrawn;
Thy wonted signs of power and grace,
   Thy power and grace are gone.

No prophet speaks to calm our woes,
   But all the seers mourn;
There's not a soul amongst us knows
   The time of thy return

Here Tate and Brady are very tired or very lazy, or else both. 'Sacred' in their sixth and again in their seventh quatrains is the merest makeweight or 'filler'. In their crucial fifth quatrain (of which more anon), not only is the rhyme 'fame'/'frame' rather plainly a desperate expedient, but the opposition between artists and the vulgar introduces a sort of class-distinction that is foreign to the original and is also – more to the point – simply distracting, since it is nowhere followed up in subsequent passages. More grievously, they commit a notable vulgarity themselves when in the last of their quatrains quoted they demote prophet to crystal-gazer. Watts is careful to avoid this, even as his introduction of 'seer' (see-er) allows for this subordinate sense of 'prophet' as fortune-teller. And of course Watts' quatrain is distinguished in another, far more important, particular: the suddenly direct colloquialism of 'There's not a soul amongst us knows'. Harry Escott's word was 'homespun', and another that hovers nearby is 'homely', which has however the unwanted possible meaning of 'unhandsome'. Better than either is George Steiner's invocation of 'a complete domestication, an at-homeness at the core'.[5] Watts' decision to rhyme twice as frequently as the New Version is, we perceive, not the empty vaunt of superior dexterity, but the sign of an altogether greater attentiveness.

Not all features of Watts' version are so immediately attractive. One takes the point when certain readers find something namby-pamby in

[5] George Steiner, *After Babel* (1975), p. 298.

'the people of his love / His little chosen flock', or again in 'Thy children in their nest'. The explanation – not an excuse, supposing excuse is called for – is surely sectarian: as a minister to the Independents (in later usage, Congregationalists), Watts was continually aware of the nonconformists' notion of 'a gathered church', a minority gathered *from* the world and therefore necessarily in tension with society at large. This is the sentiment to which Watts gave classic expression in his hymn based on the Song of Songs, 'We are a garden wall'd around'.[6] After all, his own father had suffered active persecution for his beliefs under Charles II.

Another place where we may detect sectarian bias in Watts is where he mutes so far as possible the verses telling how iconoclastic vandals had defaced the carved woodwork of the Temple. He and those he chiefly wrote for were the spiritual and sometimes the actual heirs of Cromwellian iconoclasts from the time of the Protectorate; and whereas the London congregations that Watts ministered to were wealthy enough to adorn their meeting-houses, they were chary of doing so because of scriptural injunctions not to set up graven images. Accordingly Watts passes over this as fast and as lightly as he can. The text is hard to manage in any case. In Coverdale:

He that hewed timber afore out of the thick trees: was known to bring it to an excellent work.

But now they break down all the carved work thereof: with axes and hammers.

And in the Authorized Version:

A man was famous according as he had lifted up axes upon the thick trees.

But now they break down the carved work thereof, at once, with axes and hammers.

As we have seen, Tate and Brady are like Watts in cavalierly excluding the possibility that the ancient woodmen competed publicly to see who could fell most cedars in the shortest time; though Watts cunningly allows for this, while not committing himself, in the calculated vagueness of 'he who deals the heaviest stroke / Procures the chief renown'.

This is the point however at which to take note of a later psalmodist, Christopher Smart in 1763:

6 See Donald Davie, *A Gathered Church* (1978), pp. 28–30.

> The servile hand that hew'd the wood
>   From out the stately trees
> Was, in his place, ordain'd to good,
>   And shap'd his work to please.
>
> But now these artizans untune
>   The musick that they made,
> The carvers break each fair festoon,
>   And counteract their trade.

The difficulty of the crux – baldly, how to relate the first verse to the second around the one common element, 'axe' – provokes Smart into a blaze of inventive genius. His splendid *trouvaille*, 'festoon', evokes just that carved woodwork, as by Grinling Gibbons, which Smart was as determined to celebrate as Watts was to deplore. And the wholly gratuitous parallel between one art, sculpture, and another, music, launches Smart upon speculations that we associate with twentieth-century aesthetics rather than eighteenth-century church-going: fine-drawn arguments to the effect that, just as the quarryman hewing out the marble block may be regarded as the first sculptor of that block, so the woodman who fells a tree may be seen as the first carver of its timber. Add the rich orchestration that frames the bold alliterations – 'musick . . . made' and 'fair festoon' – inside the less obvious but more potent relationships of vowels in 'artizans untune' and of consonants in 'Carvers . . . counteract', and we have verses so thoroughly *wrought* that it is surely scandalous so few readers know of them.

What are we to think when we discover that this crux which simply defeated Tate and Brady, which Watts suavely circumvented, which fired Smart to splendid invention, is merely a mistake? For so it appears. Modern scholars have decided that the Masoretic text which brings in the ancient lumbermen is corrupt, and out of Greek and Syriac versions they have come up with 'At the upper entrance they hacked the wooden trellis with axes'[7] – which is of no poetic interest whatever. Are we to conclude that Smart (and Coverdale and the King James translators before him) simply, and however excusably, mistranslated; whereas Tate and Brady, for whatever discreditable reasons, did not? The gulf between translation considered as a handmaid to erudition, and translation as imaginative endeavour, could hardly yawn more widely. Before we are through we shall have to try, like many before us, to throw a bridge over this gap.

---

[7] *The New Oxford Annotated Bible* (1965, 1977), p. 712.

Smart, belligerently Anglican, is as sectarian as Watts – to the point where, in the eleventh quatrain of his version of Psalm 74, he says the opposite of what he means to say:

> O God, how long shall traitors sting,
>   And hiss with spite and guile,
> And with th'established church and King
>   Their Saviour Christ revile?

For Smart proceeds headlong; he writes rapidly and carelessly. We can see how much more prudently Watts conducts himself at the same point:

> How long, eternal God, how long
>   Shall men of pride blaspheme!
> Shall saints be made their endless song.
>   And bear immortal shame?

The two versions are so different that it's hard to believe they have a common source – in the verse that Coverdale gives as:

> O God, how long shall the adversary do this dishonour; how long shall the enemy blaspheme thy Name, for ever?

Everything depends on how 'the adversary' or 'the enemy' is identified. For Smart, he is the old Cromwellian, perhaps by now Socinian as often as Calvinist, in either case a pretender to 'the inner Light', and probably either covertly or overtly republican; for Watts, less explicitly but just as insistently, the adversary is one of Claverhouse's troopers riding down the Covenanters. For this, so far as I can see, is how to decode Watts' 'saints'. Watts writes necessarily in code, Smart in plain speech – this is part of the difference between an anti-Establishment and an Establishment author. Because Smart's artistry is in fairly obvious ways elaborate and circuitous, 'plain' seems the wrong word for him. But if it is true he sometimes writes in a sort of code, that is of his own volition; no socio-political constraints compel him to it – only his conviction that he belongs in a cultural elite, and addresses others of that elite, in a code they have the key to. Watts on the other hand, though in principle vowed to 'the plain', uses a code because he has to. And it isn't his fault that the key to his codes has been indolently lost, even or especially by nonconformists.

The remainder of Psalm 74 comes out as follows, from the hands of Watts on the one side, of Smart on the other:

Watts	Smart
What strange deliv'rance hast thou shown,	Why dost thou our defence withdraw
In ages long before!	At this so great alarm,
– And now, no other God we own,	Nor keepest Antichrist in awe
No other God adore.	By thine almighty arm?
Thou didst divide the raging sea,	For Christ, my king from long ago,
By thy resistless might,	Is with me to this hour;
To make thy tribes a wondrous way;	All hope above, and help below,
And then secure their flight.	Are solely from his pow'r.
Is not the world of nature thine –	That pow'r astonish'd floods avow'd,
The darkness and the day?	Dividing heap from heap;
Didst thou not bid the morning shine,	Thou smote the dragons as they plough'd
And mark the sun his way?	The waters of the deep.
Hath not thy power form'd ev'ry coast,	The huge Leviathan was stunn'd
And set the earth its bounds,	At that stupendous roar
With summer's heat, and winter's frost,	Of billows, breaking to refund
In their perpetual rounds?	The fishes on the shore.
And shall the sons of earth and dust	The living springs and streams profuse
That sacred power blaspheme?	Thy people to supply,
Will not that hand which form'd them first	Thy mandate could from rocks educe,
Avenge thine injured name?	And made the river dry.
Think on the cov'nant thou hast made,	The day is subject to thy rule,
And all the words of love;	The night to thy decree,
Nor let the birds of prey invade,	The blessed sunshine and the cool
And vex thy mourning dove.	Are made and chang'd by thee.
Our foes would triumph in our blood,	Thou by thy wisdom hast ordain'd
And make our hope their jest:	The borders of the world,
Plead thine own cause, almighty God,	And summer's genial heat maintain'd
And give thy children rest.	And wintry winds unfurl'd.
	Consider, Lord, how men blaspheme
	The honour of thy name,
	And fools, in their ambitious dream
	Have lost the sense of shame.
	Let not thy turtle-dove be sold,
	To crowds and ruffian rage,
	Nor from the prostrate poor withhold
	Thy love for such an age!
	Thy gracious covenant review,
	For in this earth beneath

The worldlings dark designs pursue,
And fell revenge they breathe.

Let not the simple man depart
Abash'd at fruitless pray'r;
But give the poor a joyful heart
Thy glory to declare.

Arise, O God, thy cause support,
Thine own eternal cause,
Reclaim the folly that in sport
Contemns thy name and laws.

O let thy words of comfort drown
The voice of rank excess,
And bring their gross presumption down
To worship and to bless.

What we are likely to notice first is that from Watts' version Leviathan has been erased completely. And we may well feel mutinous: this
seems to be a translator who, whenever his original supplies an effect
in a quite narrow sense spectacular, will deny it to us. And this is
true; as John Hoyles has noted, there was never a poet who abjured
visual effects so consistently as Watts does – he excludes 'spectacle'
consistently, and on principle. Yet in the present case he was very
well advised; or rather he well advised himself. For although there is a
long tradition of identifying Leviathan with the whale (less often,
with the crocodile), and although many writers have made poetically
justifiable and sometimes delightful inventions out of that identification, the balance of probability is very much against them. After all,
the ancient Israelites were not a sea-going people. Modern scholarship sees Leviathan, or – his alternative name – Rahab, as wholly a
mythological or more precisely allegorical creature.[8] And yet, when
Watts refuses to have any truck with Leviathan, he is not prodigiously
anticipating the findings of later scholarship. It was his *poetic* intelligence that made him eliminate Leviathan because of the insuperable
difficulties it would have let him in for when he had to decide who or
what fed on the flesh of the monster, once vanquished. For the texts
are insistent, though at odds with one another. Coverdale (the
Authorized Version hardly differs) gives 'Thou smotest the heads of
Leviathan in pieces: and gavest him to be meat for the people in the
wilderness'; whereas Tate and Brady, agreeing oddly enough with *The*

[8] See *The New Oxford Annotated Bible*, p. 712: 'the monster of chaos (Leviathan or Rahab), a
personification of the restless waters of the sea'.

New Oxford Annotated, decided that those who devoured the dead Leviathan were 'savage beasts'. As Watts seems to have recognized, the difference is of no account; for the denizens of Israel, whether human or non-human, could not have survived for long on a diet of whale-meat, or crocodile-meat either. Since the creature is allegorical, so is the eating of his flesh, and in neither case do we have spectacle – on the contrary, neither dead nor alive can Leviathan be visualized. Accordingly Watts' elimination of Leviathan seems more responsible than Smart's attempt to accommodate him with legerdemain:

> Thou smote the dragons as they plough'd
>   The waters of the deep.
>
> The huge Leviathan was stunn'd
>   At that stupendous roar
> Of billows, breaking to refund
>   The fishes on the shore.

This, with its enjambement, sounds deliciously, but it appears to be quite nonsensical; at all events no sense that the *Oxford English Dictionary* gives for 'refund', including the most obsolete, seems to make sense of Smart's lines. (Robert Brittain, in an invaluable pioneer study of Smart's poetry, sees 'refund' here as an instance of Smart's Horatianism.[9] And it seems true that whereas virtually every eighteenth-century poet knew Horace and revered him – Watts certainly did – Smart's attempt to combine Roman *curiosa felicitas* with Hebrew themes and sentiments was something special. But of course this cannot be an excuse for writing nonsense.)

Scholars in general dislike making value judgements. An older generation of literary historians, still numerous and active, were sufficiently bemused by scientific scholarship to believe that their own activity could be, and was, 'value-free'. But not only did their own vocabulary quite evidently betray that they were thinking in terms of better and worse (among authors, among books), they also just as evidently relied on the acceptance of a received canon (of authors, and of books) which they were ready to revise, if at all, only timidly. A later generation has easily shown that this notion of the canonical is only a disguise for continual value judgements, mostly unargued; and these younger historians, having demonstrated this, conceive themselves to be thus

---

[9] Robert Brittain (ed.), *Poems by Christopher Smart* (Princeton, 1950), p. 70.

liberated into a pursuit that shall be, once again and more authentic-
ally, value-free.

But with translations the case is different. For as regards translations,
there never has been a canon; no one translation of a text has ever, or at
least not for long, been thought more canonical than any other. The
most compelling proof of this is Pope's Homer: a monumental translation by a poet of acknowledged genius (and *there's* a value judgement), it has never been forgotten and yet never, from Pope's day to
ours, has it been thought pre-eminent among available versions of
Homer. Translations may be sorted according as they are 'faithful' or
'unfaithful' (a distinction usually confounded with a quite different and
equally muddled opposition of the 'literal' to the 'free'), but hardly
anyone has thought that these terms provide a basis either for extolling
Pope's *Iliad* or for discounting it. And 'fidelity' itself is a tool that comes
to pieces in our hands as soon as we try to make use of it. There is no
canon of translations into English, no array of translations that can be
called 'classic', because there has never been agreement about what
criteria a translation should be judged by. Accordingly, if we ask which
translation of Psalm 74 is the better – Watts' or Smart's – we are at a loss
to know how to proceed. And if we think, as most of us probably do,
that either of these versions is superior to Nahum Tate's, we seem to
have no way of proving that either.

However, out of recent translation theory there has emerged one
paradigm which seems subtler than anything before, and yet manage-
able. This is George Steiner's model by which every act of imaginative
translation has four aspects, or proceeds through four phases. These are:
(1) trust, (2) aggression, (3) incorporation, (4) restitution.[10] What
Steiner means by each of these terms will emerge if we take them one by
one and apply them to Watts' and Smart's renderings of Psalm 74.

Trust means in the first place the translator's trust that in the foreign
text there is something valuable enough to deserve the pains he must
take to release it. Most journeymen or commercially commissioned
translations fail to meet this first test, and of course we may suspect –
though unfairly, because we cannot prove it – that Tate's is a journey-
man version in this sense. With Watts and Smart, however, there can be
no such doubt; for both of them the Psalms were Holy Writ, and
a proper understanding of them was unnecessary to salvation. What
was of value in them was *wisdom*, and that is what both translators

10 George Steiner, *After Babel* (1975), pp. 296–303.

undertook to unlock, with the necessary implication that their predecessors (who for Smart included Watts) had failed to do so. Closely
related and yet distinct is the translator's trust, not just in the text he
translates but in the author behind that text – a person for whom he has
fellow-feeling extending in some cases to something not far short of
identification. Because King David the Psalmist is a complex figure
(how far legendary, how far historical, need not concern us), he can be
envisaged differently by different translators; and it can be inferred
that, whereas for Smart David is the king of a settled kingdom, for
Watts he is the chieftain of a small and embattled tribe menaced on all
its frontiers by more powerful neighbours.

Aggression is what Steiner very valuably makes much of. To translate
a text is to do it violence, and taking liberties with it is an inherent
necessity. As Steiner says, 'The translator invades, extracts, and brings
home.' Both Watts and Smart are keenly aware of this, and impenitent
about it, as we see from their prefatory remarks and indeed from their
very titles.[11] (Smart's is *Translation of the Psalms of David, Attempted in the
Spirit of Christianity, and Adapted to the Divine Service.*) When Watts drops
the ancient lumbermen and also Leviathan, he is doing no more
violence to the original than Smart does when *per contra* he elaborates so
as to make explicit what in the original is gnomic. Watts' conciseness –
he does in seventeen quatrains what costs Smart twenty-four – is itself
aggressive, though it surely counts in his favour.

Of *incorporation* we have spoken already when we applauded Watts'
'There's not a soul amongst us knows'. He achieves it again, strikingly,
in his last two lines. A comparable moment for Smart comes in his
twentieth quatrain:

> Nor from the prostrate poor withhold
> Thy love for such an age

where 'for such an age' is the colloquial usage that means 'for ever so
long'. But as Steiner acknowledges, it is possible to succeed all too well
with 'incorporation'. For the whole aim of translating, when it is
undertaken in all seriousness, is to reach out and encompass a foreign
body; and to do that the target-language must be strained. If it is not
put under strain beyond its normal capacities, it can never be enriched
by translation, as it ought to be. English or whatever other target-
language must be stretched to accommodate perceptions either not

---

[11] They were not the first. They had been anticipated at least in part by Archbishop Parker in
The Whole Psalter (1557?) and by John Patrick in 1679.

native to it, or once native but fallen into disuse. This is why Pound in some of his most ambitious translations – for instance, of Cavalcanti – deliberately archaized. Whether through archaisms or in some other way the strain, the stretching, has to *show*; the foreign novelty must be allowed its foreignness, its bracing or disconcerting strangeness. And it is here, surely, that Watts' peremptory elimination of Leviathan can be thought discreditable. The allegorical monster could have been handled in an idiom, 'Gothick' or Spenserian, which had long fallen out of use in the early-Hanoverian English that Watts was writing in. Forty years later, when Smart bent himself to the task, the Spenserian idiom was being tentatively rehabilitated; but Smart took no advantage of that – as we have seen, trying to domicile Leviathan in a Horatian idiom, he fell on his face. But he was right to try, and Watts was wrong not to. We might even argue that the comical wrongness of what Smart tries to do with Leviathan at least signals how the ancient Hebrew remained, in certain matters, irreducibly foreign to the Hanoverian Christians who through the agency of their poets were trying to accommodate it. Watts' version suggests on the contrary that the accommodation, the domestication, could be easy and complete.

Finally, *restitution*. The easiest case of this occurs when a translator, guiltily aware of what in the original he has scanted or been defeated by compensates for that by supplying splendours out of his own store so as to balance the books on the transaction. This is surely what Smart does, consciously or not, when he elaborates on the matter of the vandals in the Temple:

> But now these artizans untune
>   The musick that they made,
> The carvers break each fair festoon,
>   And counteract their trade.

These verses are not equivalent to any in the original; they offer themselves as penitential repayment for the wrongs that at other points the original has had to suffer.

'Restitution' can take subtler and more abject forms than this. One – favoured by some of the more responsible modern translators – is to omit, or to represent only by asterisks, those portions of the original for which the translator can find no acceptable equivalent. Here the restitution consists in the implicit acknowledgment that the original has depths which the translator has not been able to plumb. The same sort of restitution is made when the translator provides a version that is, in some of its details, nonsensical or impenetrably opaque – as seems to be the case with Pound's version of Cavalcanti's *Donna mi prega*, which became Canto 36.

However, these are modernist strategies that we must admit were not in practical terms available to eighteenth-century poets like Watts and Smart. As between these two, Steiner's model enables us, I think, to give the palm to Smart because (1) his 'incorporation' is less deceptively complete than Watts'; (2) his 'restitution' is more bountiful. Of course, if we compared them on the score of another Psalm, our judgement might go the other way.

It may be asked what has been achieved by this exercise. Who cares whether one metrical version of a Psalm is better or worse than another? One can only reply that we are dealing with two greatly gifted and devout poets, and that the text on which they exert themselves is one of the fundamental texts of Christendom – of Jewry also, but that is another story. The passing of value judgements is not an unwarranted intrusion on texts from our past; on the contrary, it is what they implicitly demand, and deserve.

7

Inwardness and the dictionary

In something so familiar to most of us as 'Hark! the herald angels sing', we sing what seems, on a little reflection, nonsense:

> Hail the Heaven-born Prince of Peace!
> Hail the Sun of Righteousness!
> Light and life to all He brings,
> Risen with healing in His wings.

Since when did a sun have wings? And if it did have them, on the experience of the only sun we know of physically, those wings would bring pestilence as often as healing. Is this a reasonable objection? There are those – not poets, however – who will protest that such prosaic commonsense is out of place when we approach poetry. A better defence, from a quite different direction, is that Wesley is being scriptural:

> But unto you that feare my Name shall the Sunne of righteousness arise with healing in his wings. (Malachi 4.2)

And yet not all scriptural texts speak with equal authority. Contrast 2 Samuel 23.4, one of the older Scriptures that the author of Malachi is thought to be alluding to at this point:

> And he shall be as the light of the morning, when the Sunne riseth, even a morning, without cloudes; as the tender grass springing out of the earth by cleare shining after raine.

Here – it is a text that Cowper was to rework beautifully in 'Sometimes a light surprises' – there is none of the difficulty that we find in Malachi, which Wesley if anything aggravates: this Sun is not winged, and is recognizably the physically rising sun that Israelite shepherds could greet with relief and gratitude. Wesley is much further from sympathizing with that simple and earthily understandable response than is the author of 2 Samuel, who conveys the healing by implication in his image of the tender and springing grass.

And yet perhaps we should be grateful. For Malachi 4.2 reads in full in the Authorized Version:

> But unto you that feare my Name, shall the Sunne of righteousness arise with healing in his wings, and shall goe forth and grow up as calves of the staule.

It seems we may be grateful that Charles Wesley, having envisaged a sun with wings, did not go on to identify this with calves in, or exuberantly released from, their stalls in a byre. Mixed metaphor is still mixed, though we encounter it in Scripture. And the literal-minded Wesley is not thinking in or through metaphor at all; because what he focusses on in a metaphor is its *tenor*, never its *vehicle*.

These are semi-technical terms. But the sense of them is straight-forward when we review Watts' and Christopher Smart's dealings with Psalm 74. The *tenor*, the general bearing and intention, of the Psalmist's metaphors is clear to Watts and Smart, as it is to all of us. What they wrestle with is the *vehicle*: just how are woodmen felling trees in Lebanon connected with iconoclasts defacing the Temple? Is God's 'turtle-dove' caged and up for sale, or roaming free? Above all, who is 'Leviathan', and by whom or what is he eaten when God has van-quished him? It is the making sense on a literal level, the avoidance of mixed metaphor, that taxes the translators; whereas Wesley avoids these difficulties simply by refusing to recognize them.

This is a sweeping judgement, and to make it stick we ideally need to prove that this way of proceeding was with Wesley habitual – some-thing that, with an author so copious, is next to impossible. It is to the point, however, that instances of it are not limited to Wesley's poetry but can be found in his prose, and prose intended in the first place for no eye but his own. We find it in his Journal for 25 July 1743, where he is reporting on his turbulent evangelizing mission to West Cornwall:

> *Mon., 25th July.* The Mayor told us, that the Ministers were the principal authors of all this evil, by continually representing us in their sermons as Popish emissaries, and urging the enraged multitude to take all manner of ways to stop us. Their whole preaching is cursings and lies; yet they modestly say, my fellow-labourer and I are the cause of all the disturbance. It is always the lamb that troubles the water.[1]

---

[1] John R. Tyson (ed.), *Charles Wesley. A Reader* (New York, 1989), p. 245.

That last sentence is effectively sarcastic. Yet its being cast in the form of a proverb or an adage shows how it can be nothing of the kind. It has nothing to do with the behaviour of sheep or their lambs close to water. The lamb is an *emblematic* lamb; and the water is emblematic water.

A Dante scholar has suggested to me that objections like this which we make about Wesley could as well be levelled at the author of *The Divine Comedy*. And it is surely true that the grotesque effects we find in the Book of Revelation and in some hymns by Wesley – roughly, an image or a series of images that cannot be visualized – seem to have been deliberately sought out by Dante at certain crucial points in his all-inclusive poem. Recognizing that much, we might embark on a rather elaborate distinction between the allegorical imagination and the metaphorical. But for our purposes it is enough to register the possibility that there survived in Charles Wesley, a child of the Enlightenment, recognizably mediaeval habits of thought and imagination.

The oddity of this will not come clear until we recognize Wesley as a child of the Enlightenment in a sense not merely chronological. And this will be resisted, not least by those who conceive of the Enlightenment as essentially and by definition irreligious. But Wesley's verse quite often strikes notes that make it thoroughly at home in its age:

> Entring on Life's Meridian Stage
> I see the Shades appear,
> And feel Anticipated Age,
> Death's welcome Harbinger,[2]

There will be those who find this quatrain stilted and frosty. But surely on the contrary it is marmoreal: as a mordantly succinct observation on middle age, it might be carved in marble. (The off-rhyme, I would say, helps rather than hinders.) It is, or seems to be, memorably imperturbable, in the manner of an unbelieving stoic. And just here we come upon the strangeness: that the author of these seemingly imperturbable verses was very perturbed indeed – by nightmare visions reaching back through the Middle Ages to apocalyptic parts of Scripture. In him it seems we find a Gothic imagination struggling inside an Augustan carapace.

And yet, make what allowances we may and must to this special case, do we not have to decide that Charles Wesley was an inferior poet to

---

[2] S. T. Kimbrough Jr and Oliver A. Beckerlegge, *The Unpublished Poetry of Charles Wesley, Volume I* (Nashville, 1988), p. 259.

Watts and Smart, because an inferior *kind* of poet? Before we can arrive at such a valuation, Wesley must be given another run for our money. Consider accordingly his treatment of Psalm 137.

This is the poignantly compact poem that begins, in Coverdale's Prayer-book version:

> By the waters of Babylon we sat down and wept: when we remembered thee, O Sion.

The next verse has entered into an entirely secular tradition:

> I'll hang my harp on a weeping willow tree,
> And may the world go well with thee.

And then there comes the matter of the jeering victors requiring that the vanquished and exiled sing something redolent of their vanished home:

> For they that led us away captive required of us then a song, and melody, in our heaviness: Sing us one of the songs of Sion.

The succeeding verses (4 to 6) movingly declare how, if their mouths complied with the order, their hearts remained devoted to Jerusalem.

What it is less convenient to remember is how the Psalm ends, in a spasm of vindictive vengefulness, quite specific, that cannot be argued away:

> O daughter of Babylon, wasted with misery:
> yea, happy shall he be that rewardeth thee, as thou hast served us.
> Blessed shall he be that taketh thy children:
> and throweth them against the stones.

The Authorized Version, giving 'dasheth' for 'throweth', is even less ambiguous.

Christopher Smart, avowedly reading the Old Testament in the light of the New, cannot countenance the atrocity:

> Renown'd the man! that shall reward
> And serve thee as thou'st serv'd the Lord,
>   Thou shalt thy turn deplore;
> There's desolation too for thee,
> Thou daughter of calamity,
>   And Babylon no more!
>
> But he is greatest and the best,
> Who spares his enemies profest,
>   And Christian mildness owns;

> Who gives his captives back their lives,
> Their helpless infants, weeping wives,
> And for his sin atones.[3]

But Wesley cannot be so compassionate:

> Surely our God shall Vengeance take
> On these that gloried in our Faith.
> He a full End of Sin shall make,
> Of all that held our Souls in Thrall;
> O *Babylon*, Thy Day shall come.
> Prepare to meet Thy final Doom.
>
> Happy, the Man that see in Thee
> The mystic *Babylon* within;
> And fill'd with Holy Cruelty
> Disdains to spare that smallest Sin,
> And sternly takes Thy little Ones,
> And dashes all against the Stones.

By placing the atrocious drama 'within', and declaring Babylon 'mystic', Wesley can duck away from the hideousness of what he is saying: the 'little ones', the babies, are notional or emblematic; and so are the stones against which their brains are dashed out. The poetic or rhetorical procedure validates, or is taken to validate, an ethical procedure that is inexcusable – as Smart for one, among Wesley's contemporaries, seems to have recognized. 'Holy Cruelty' is, one way or another, a memorable expression.

Wesley's 'Psalm 137 Paraphrased'[4] is an unfortunate performance all through. For instance the verse that supplied the refrain to 'There is a tavern in the town' ('As for our harps', says Coverdale, 'we hanged them up: upon the trees that are therein') elicited from Wesley:

> Our Harps no longer vocal now,
> We cast aside untuned, unstrung,
> Forgot them pendent on the Bough:
> Let meaner Sorrows find a tongue,
> Silent we sat, and scorn'd relief,
> In all the majesty of grief.

---

[3] Norman Callan (ed.), *The Collected Poems of Christopher Smart* (London, 1949), vol. 2, p. 756.
[4] John R. Tyson (ed.), *Charles Wesley. A Reader*, p. 403. The MS is in Westminster College, Cambridge.

If the quatrain on middle age ('Entring on Life's Meridian Stage') gives us mid-eighteenth-century verse at something near its best, this surely represents it at its worst: not only intolerably diffuse, but also *tumid* in the sense that Byron intended when in *English Bards and Scotch Reviewers* (1809) he wrote of 'Turgid ode and tumid stanza'. Moreover, if we remember Martha Winburn England saying that Wesley as poet was 'vulgar', we surely encounter that vulgarity with 'In all the majesty of grief'. In the Psalmist, as in Coverdale following him, we detect such 'majesty' precisely because it is left to be inferred; as soon as Wesley all too explicitly claims it, it vanishes. For a grieving person does not look aside from his grief so as to claim majesty for it. And this is in line with Wesley's treatment of the Sun of Righteousness: time and again he insists on making explicit what in his originals – for instance in this case the passage from 2 Samuel – is left implicit. He does not trust the implications of image and metaphor. It does nothing for our opinion of 'Psalm 137 Paraphrased' to discover that the Babylon at whom this polemic is directed is nothing more potent or menacing than the Methodists who wanted to break with the Church of England, whereas Charles and his associates were determined they should not:

> O England's desolate Church, if Thee,
>   Tho' desolate, I remember not,
> Let me, when lost to Piety,
>   Be lost myself and clean forgot.
> Cleave to the Roof my speechless Tongue,
> When *Sion* is not all my song!

Is it then dissident Methodists whose children are to be dashed against stones? Not really; for such dashing, and indeed such children, are to be understood only as 'within', as 'mystic'.

Wesley's 'within' appeals to a realm of *inwardness* which the devout in all denominations know to be a reality. The concept did not originate with the Methodists, nor has it ever been peculiar to them. It has undoubtedly supported many honest people in their devotions, and still does. Poetically, however, it opens up a minefield; and not only nor chiefly because it can lead unbalanced individuals to fantasize about killing other people's children, while assuring themselves they are doing nothing of the sort. For a language is public property; and inwardness, the 'inner light' that the oldest dissenters insisted on, makes it private, to the point where extremists can think that words mean what they want them to mean, despite what the dictionary may say to the contrary. This may be thought to be a special version of the hoary heresy called antinomian. If so, antinomianism is alive and well, in quarters not touched by Christian belief but much concerned (theoretically) with reading and writing.

Here indeed we surely reach a point where the language of religious devotion and the language of poetry may diverse, drastically. Though many have thought otherwise, estimable poetry sets its face against what Wesley called 'mystic'. It has to do so, to meet its obligations to language as public currency, answerable to the dictionary. 'Lamb' means a young sheep; and 'cruelty' means *cruelty*, however we may out of our inwardness qualify it with epithets like 'holy'. To be sure the dictionaries, at least if we begin with Johnson's (1755), can be seen, along with all other literary works that ever exerted influence, as instruments of class domination, of coercion. It is possible to read the entire body of English hymnody in this reductive fashion, as Lionel Adey does.[5] But this is a conspiracy theory, according to which innumerable well-meaning people were, quite without their knowing it, being manipulated by a higher power either secular or, in more ambitious versions, metaphysical though irreligious ('manifest destiny', 'the logic of history'). What is to be made of the fact that Commodore Perry USN, on his second visit to Japan in 1854, caused the ship's company on his flagship to sing, to the tune of the *Old Hundredth*, Doddridge's hymn, 'Hark the glad sound! the Saviour comes'?[6] Is this to convict Philip Doddridge of being an American imperialist *avant la lettre*? The notion is, in the strictest sense, preposterous; it reads into the past motives that persons in the past could not have entertained, even unconsciously. And obviously the same goes for lexicographers like Samuel Johnson who, it so happens, explicitly deplored French and English imperialism in North America. Thus, to appeal to the dictionary (to a great dictionary like Johnson's or Sir James Murray's *Oxford English Dictionary*) is not to appeal to 'received opinion'. The appeal is to a court more nearly objective than any other available to literary study or literary composition.

And this appeal must be made particularly on behalf of public devotions. For if the criterion of inwardness is pushed to its limit, it reduces public devotions – communal worship – to at most marginal status: if inwardness is the measure, then the only true devotion is private – public worship represents at best a point of intersection

[5] Lionel Adey, *Class and Idol in the English Hymn* (Vancouver, 1988).
[6] Tyler Whittle, *Solid Joys and Lasting Treasure* (Bolton, 1985), p. 41.

between various private fervours and peroccupations. The authors of congregational hymns suppose on the contrary that devotion is real only in so far as it is shared. In this way, the cultural achievement represented by a great dictionary, and the religious achievement represented by an accepted rite of worship, lock together.

Charles Wesley's life-long struggle not to be forced out of the Church of England suggests that he recognized this importance of rite, with its set forms; and equally there are verses of his which exhibit what Ezra Pound admired in the verse of Johnson, 'the lexicographer's weighing of the epithet'. Undoubtedly, however, there are usages in his verse which point quite elsewhere.

1. Detail of plaque, St Anne's Church, Manchester.

2. Plaque to John Byrom in his birthplace, Manchester.

3. Francis Hayman, *Self-Portrait at the Easel*, 1750.

4. Louis François Roubiliac, bust by Jonathan Tyers.

5. Thomas Stocking, rococo plasterwork in Royal Fort House, Bristol, c. 1760.

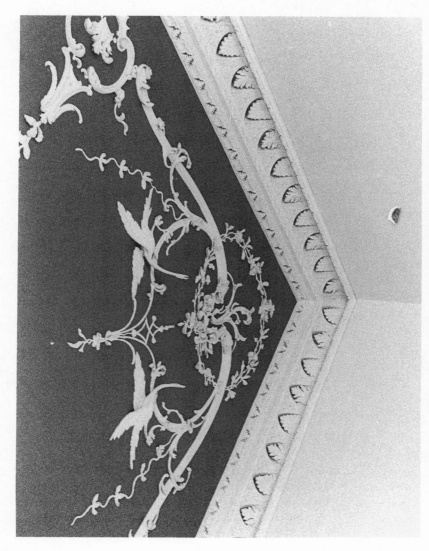

6. Thomas Stocking, rococo plasterwork on ceiling of Royal Fort House, Bristol, c. 1760.

7. Thomas Stocking, rococo decoration, Royal Fort House, Bristol, c. 1760.

8

Christopher Smart and English rococo

In Chapter IX of that small classic, J. T. Smith's *Nollekens and His Times* (2 vols. 1828, Turnstile Press, 1949), Smith remarks:

great as Hogarth was in his display of every variety of character, I should never think of exhibiting a portfolio of his prints to the youthful inquirer; nor can I agree that the man who was so accustomed to visit, so fond of delineating, and who gave up so much of his time to the vices of the most abandoned classes, was in truth a 'moral teacher of mankind'. My father knew Hogarth well, and I have often heard him declare, that he revelled in the company of the drunken and profligate: Churchill, Wilkes, Hayman, etc., were among his constant companions.

However, this boon companionship was certainly dissolved by 1764 when Churchill in his 'Gotham' (I.367–76) went out of his way to abuse the painter Francis ('Frank') Hayman:

> The months twelve sisters, all of different hue,
> Though there appears in all a likeness too;
> Not such a likeness, as, through Hayman's works,
> Dull mannerist! in Christians, Jews, and Turks,
> Cloys with a sameness in each female face ...

And the reason is not far to seek: Churchill, as Wilkes' friend, is striking at Hayman, who was Hogarth's. For Hogarth and Wilkes had quarreled, initially on the score of Hogarth's 1762 engraving, 'The Times', which was seen, and no doubt rightly, as supporting the young George III and his mother's favourite the Earl of Bute against William Pitt and the whigs who had conducted the Seven Years' War with France. Wilkes, whig and Pittite, at once retaliated. 'Hogarth, Sergeant Painter to the King since 1757, was condemned as the lackey of royal policy.'[1] And Churchill had weighed in with his characteristic brutality, in

---

[1] William Gaunt, *The World of William Hogarth* (1978), pp. 113–14.

'Epistle to William Hogarth', where he affects to believe that Hogarth is senile:

> Sure 'tis a curse which angry fates impose,
> To mortify man's arrogance, that those
> Who're fashion'd of some better sort of clay,
> Much sooner than the common herd decay.
> What bitter pangs must humbled Genius feel,
> In their last hours to view a Swift and Steele!
> How must ill-boding horrors fill her breast,
> When she beholds men mark'd above the rest
> For qualities most dear, plunged from that height,
> And sunk, deep sunk, in second childhood's night!
> Are men, indeed, such things? and are the best
> More subject to this evil than the rest,
> To drivel out whole years of idiot breath,
> And sit the monuments of living death?
> Oh, galling circumstance to human pride!
> Abasing thought, but not to be denied!
> With curious art the brain, too finely wrought,
> Preys on herself, and is destroy'd by thought.
> Constant attention wears the active mind,
> Blots out her powers, and leaves a blank behind.
> But let not youth, to insolence allied,
> In heat of blood, in full career of pride,
> Possess'd of genius, with unhallow'd rage
> Mock the infirmities of reverend age:
> The greatest genius to this fate may bow;
> Reynolds, in time, may be like Hogarth now.

Brutal though he is, Churchill manages this close extremely well, surprising us with what seems eleventh-hour magnanimity.

Christopher Smart had been for years on good terms with Hogarth, and on better, even intimate, terms with Francis Hayman. Yet he need not have been embroiled in this falling out among drinking companions (of whom, in his bibulous years, he may have been one), except for one circumstance: whereas Hogarth's losing his wits was a baseless rumour, Smart had in 1763 just emerged from several years in a private mad-house, as was well known. And so the anonymous reviewer of his collection of that year knew where to strike:

But we will say no more of Mr. Smart; Peace be to the *manes* of his departed muse. Our sentiments with regards to this unfortunate gentleman are such as every man must feel on the same melancholy occasion. If our readers are desirous to know what they are, we must refer them to the fine lines at the end of Mr. Churchill's epistle to Hogarth.[2]

The pity is that Churchill's verses are indeed 'fine'; fine enough to make us wonder if in this famous altercation (for it went on, Hogarth hitting back with biting caricatures of both Wilkes and Churchill), there is not after all more than mere spite and splenetic party politics.

Is there for instance any substance to the objection that Churchill raises to Hayman's painting – his not differentiating between one female face and the next? Differentiation, individuation, is not after all so much of a requisite according to some art theories as it is in others. Might we not retort to Churchill by asking whether his 'youth, to insolence allied' is *individuated*; and whether, if it had been, it could have served the driving purpose that Churchill had in mind for it? There are some aesthetic systems which, so far from setting store by individuation, positively deplore it; and Hayman may have painted according to such an aesthetic.

Francis Hayman (1708–76) was no inconsiderable figure. Not just in the estimation of his own time, but in present-day perspectives also, he is a figure substantial enough for Churchill's querulousness about him to have more than a 'period' interest.[3] Born at Exeter and apprenticed to the history painter Robert Brown, on his removal to London he was first employed as a scenery painter at Drury Lane. But he became famous through his decorative paintings for Vauxhall Gardens, through which he seems to have become known to Smart, who may have struck up acquaintance with the Vauxhall Gardens artists (musicians and sculptors as well as painters) even before he left Cambridge for London in 1749. Meanwhile Hayman, who worked closely with Hogarth on the Vauxhall Gardens project, had been with him on the visit to France in 1748 which produced Hogarth's fiercely anti-Gallican 'The Gate of Calais', better known from the engraving, 'O The Roast Beef of Old England' (1749). Though other members of the party travelled on to Flanders and Holland, Hayman with Hogarth was briefly detained on the suspicion that they were English spies. In later years Hayman, a notable *bon viveur*, parted from Hogarth in actively working for a professional association of English artists such as was ultimately realized in the Royal Academy.

---

[2] *Critical Review XVI* (November, 1763), p. 395. Quoted by Arthur Sherbo, *Christopher Smart. Scholar of the University* (Michigan, 1967), p. 188.

[3] See Brian Allen, *Francis Hayman* (New Haven and London, 1987).

Hayman, much in demand as an illustrator after collaborating with Gravelot on Hanmer's six-volume edition of Shakespeare (1743–4), illustrated Smart's *Poems on Several Occasions* (1752).[4] Smart named him in 'The Blockhead and Beehive' (c. 1754 – "Till Hayman's matchless art despairs'); and later in the song, 'Where shall Caelia fly for shelter?':

> Cupid shoots like Hayman's archer
> Wheresoe'er the damsel turns.

(Hayman had painted 'An archer and a landscape' for Vauxhall Gardens; there may be a pun on Hayman/Hymen.) Smart praised him too in *The Midwife* (II.279) and called him 'my friend' in *The Student* (I.249).[5] The two men were fellow-members of several convivial clubs. But the crucial link between them was surely Vauxhall Gardens which, originally a public resort of the Restoration under the name of Spring Gardens, was reopened in 1732 by the impresario Jonathan Tyers (d. 1767), whom Smart commemorated in *Jubilate Agno*.

For, according to Sir Roy Strong (*The Sunday Times Magazine*, 19 November 1989), Vauxhall Gardens, as devised by Tyers on the advice of Hogarth, was 'a rococo paradise', and 'the perfect expression in this country of the rococo, a style ideally suited to the architecture of transitory pleasures, to gardens, mascarades and theatre'. Sure enough, whereas rococo crops up, though never without some unease, in accounts of early Hogarth, it is insisted on in nearly all accounts of Hayman. The latter's 'Wrestling Scene from "As You Like It"' is called 'one of the most graceful English interpretations of the French Rococo style', and we are told that 'his French-influenced Rococo style was readily absorbed by the young Gainsborough'.[6] Other authorities, like the massively learned Frederick Antal,[7] tend to shift the credit for introducing rococo to England from Hayman to his French collaborator Hubert Gravelot, properly Hubert Francois Bourguignon (1699–1773, in England 1732/3–45). 'Hayman in particular was impressed by the rococo elegance of Gravelot's work, an object lesson in refinement that modified insular roughness.'[8] But however that may be, and though Gravelot rather than Hayman may be credited with introduc-

---

[4] His frontispiece, referring to Smart's 'The Hop Garden', is reproduced by Karina Williamson in *The Poetical Works of Christopher Smart* (vol. IV, Oxford, 1987).

[5] Arthur Sherbo, *Christopher Smart. Scholar of the University* (Michigan, 1967), p. 61.

[6] Elizabeth Einberg and Judy Egerton, *The Age of Hogarth. British Painters born 1675–1709* (The Tate Gallery, 1988), pp. 40, 43.

[7] Frederick Antal, *Hogarth and his Place in European Art* (1962).

[8] William Gaunt, *The World of William Hogarth* (1978), p. 45.

ing rococo first to Hogarth and then to Gainsborough, it remains true
that Smart after 1750 associated with artists, pre-eminently Hayman,
for whom the label rococo has seemed appropriate. If a weightier name
than Hayman's is called for, it could be – if not Hogarth's, which was in
Smart's mind when he wrote *Jubilate Agno* – then that of the sculptor
Louis François Roubiliac (?1705–62; in England from c. 1732). Though
as with Hogarth so with Roubiliac, art historians are understandably
reluctant, faced with inventive genius, to invoke a category so seemingly constricting and frivolous as rococo, yet Roubiliac's audaciously
unbuttoned effigy of Handel, commissioned by Tyers for Vauxhall and
now in the Victoria and Albert Museum, cannot help being taken, by
Roy Strong and others, as sounding the keynote for what the Vauxhall
Gardens artists were called upon to do. And Smart duly genuflected:

> Like statues made by Roubilliac
> Tho' form'd beyond all skill antique
>
> (Madam and the Magpie, 1767)

and, more pertinently (claiming kinship by marriage):

> Not He whose highly finish'd piece
> Outshone the chisell'd forms of Greece;
> Who found with all his art and fame
> A partner in the house I claim.
>
> (Epistle to John Sherratt, 1763)

Smart associated with, if indeed he did not identify with, artists of
English rococo; the question arises whether, in his practice of his own
art of poetry, he did not subscribe to a rococo aesthetic.

But this, the aesthetics of rococo, is nowhere to be found. Hogarth's
Analysis of Beauty (1753), though it repeatedly and intriguingly promises
as much, in the end fails to deliver. So one falls back on the handbooks.
In their *Dictionary of Art and Artists* (1959; reprinted with revisions
1987), Peter and Linda Murray seem to be grumpy about rococo in any
case. They avoid using the term in their entries for Hayman and
Roubiliac, and they declare, in a tone that sounds self-satisfied, that
'England did not take to Rococo and in France it fell out of fashion in
the 1740s.' Accordingly, they offer not a definition, only a description:

Rococo – which comes from a French word *rocaille*, meaning rock-work – is
basically a style of interior decoration, and consists principally in the use of C
scrolls and counter-curves, and, in its fullest form around 1730, asymmetrical

arrangements of curves in panelling and elsewhere... The characteristics of small curves, prettiness and gaiety, can also be found in painting and sculpture of the period – Watteau and Boucher, and even, in a very modified form, in Hogarth.

Required to find, in the verbal art of poetry, analogues of 'C scrolls and counter-curves, and ... asymmetrical arrangements of curves', we may well retire defeated and abashed, persuaded that our perception of common ground between a poet and his contemporaries in painting, sculpture and architecture must be the merest impressionism.

Yet we may note that forty or fifty years ago the same situation obtained concerning the term 'baroque'. In Sir Paul Harvey's *Oxford Companion to English Literature* (2nd edn, 1937), there is no intimation that the term 'baroque' ever had been, or could be, applied to the literary arts. Yet in *A Dictionary of Modern Critical Terms* (1973, revised 1987), 'baroque' is allowed to have some currency in literary history. Michael Hollington, who writes the brief essay for his general editor, Roger Fowler, remains very wary: 'baroque' is, he says, 'a term denoting a distinctive style deeply characteristic of the seventeenth century, long since firmly established for critics of art and music, whose usefulness for literary critics must still be regarded as problematic and controversial'. Art historians, Hollington tells us, 'generally now agree to regard the Baroque as the third Renaissance style, setting in around 1600, with its centre in Rome and its quintessential representative in Bernini, and with important Catholic and post-tridentine tendencies'; whereas 'musicologists associate the Baroque with the advent of Monteverdi, the birth of operatic recitative and the *concertante* style, and with figured bass'. The carry-over of this concept into the history of poetry is, Hollington warns us again, fraught with difficulty: John Donne's poetry, for instance, which has been called 'baroque', should more properly be called 'mannerist' – mannerism being a mode or style lately isolated by art historians to denote what happened between high Renaissance and Baroque, or between Michelangelo and Bernini. Moreover there is current, it seems, an expression, 'Contemporary Baroque', which is sometimes used to herd under one umbrella such current story-tellers as John Barth, Iris Murdoch and Gunther Grass. Hollington will have none of this: 'The best Baroque art – the work of Bernini, Rembrandt, Milton, Monteverdi and Bach – is of a different order of intensity and coherent grandeur altogether, and one should not readily assume its recurrence.' With that adoption of Milton into the company of Bernini and Rembrandt, Monteverdi and Bach, Michael

Hollington seems to have conceded, despite all his misgivings, that 'baroque' is a term that may be, and perhaps must be, applied to some poetry in English.

For rococo (*Modern Critical Terms* has no entry under this head) one may claim no more and no less. Indeed, taking Hollington's point that the baroque is a style 'deeply characteristic of the seventeenth century', one may legitimately find it in some hymns by Isaac Watts but not, where Robert Brittain thought he found it, in hymns by Smart,[9] nor, where Vincent Newey thought he found it, in a hymn by Cowper.[10] What is at issue is more than pedantic classification; if we need rococo for the effect of Smart's poetic diction, that is because Smart's diction affects us quite differently from that of his baroque or Palladian predecessors, not to speak of his Romantic successors. On simply chronological grounds rococo seems the word that best defines that difference. And Charles Churchill's seemingly facile sneer at Francis Hayman may in the end define that difference better than more fine-drawn and philosophical discussions.

Harriet Guest for instance supplies an admirably careful reading of a stanza from Smart's *Song to David* which tells how David takes attentive care of one among the ranks of creatures:

> Of beasts – the beaver plods his task;
> While the sleek tygers roll and bask,
>   Nor yet the shades arouse:
> Her cave the mining coney scoops;
> Where o'er the mead the mountain stoops,
>   The kids exult and brouse.

Dr Guest comments:

Here the relative times and spaces indicated by 'while' and 'yet' and 'where' seem to describe a syntactical continuity which establishes the specificity of the beaver and tiger, or coney and kid, but defines their temporal and spatial positions in relation to an evasive symbolic topography. The beasts are, as it were, caught in a moment of suspended animation, in which the very particularity of the verbs they govern seems to guarantee their timelessness. Thus, the beaver's intent, as he 'plods', seems to express an enduring and substantial characteristic, rather than, or as well as, a particular aim, just as the sense in which 'the mountain stoops' describes a permanent inclination, rather than a specific intent or finite task. This kind of slippage between the particular and

9 Robert Brittain (ed.), *Poems by Christopher Smart* (Princeton, 1950), Introduction, p. 74: 'His art is the art of the baroque ... '
10 Vincent Newey, *Cowper's Poetry. A Critical Study and Reassessment* (Liverpool, 1982), p. 296.

the collective, the transitory and enduring act, is in part a function of the absence or elusiveness of the perceiving subject, or of the difficulty of determining, in these passages of the poem, whether we read David's poetry, or an account of it. In comparison to, say, the classical landscape of Pope's introduction to *Windsor-Forest*, where the repeated use of 'here' and 'there' establishes a topographical structure familiar from landscape painting, this poetry presents a series of emblematic pictures whose syntactical relations resemble rather the formal structures which lend an overall unity to the panels of a stained-glass window.[11]

What Harriet Guest is saying, if we amplify her analogy of the stained-glass window to comprehend the stonework or paint-work surrounding it, is that Smart's beaver and tiger, his coney and kid, each occupies a lunette, in Jonathan Richardson's sense when he wrote in 1722: 'The pictures are painted in a sort of Lunettes, form'd by a Semicircle within a Tall Arch ending in a Point.' Modern usage would substitute for 'lunette' the in fact less well attested 'vignette'. In either case what we have is animals frozen into a characteristic posture (though is it characteristic of beavers that they *plod*?),[12] encased in abstracted linear designs which wreathe about them. Such is for instance the design for the staircase hall at the Royal Fort in Bristol, where Thomas Stocking contrived (c. 1760) that 'cluster-laden vines rise as waving lines unsupported by a trellis', and 'at the foot of each is a charming pastoral scene distinguished from its neighbours by its animal occupants – a dog, fox, ducks on a pond, sheep, birds, and squirrels resting or disporting in the upper branches'.[13] Though there are still readers who think they find in Smart's poetry reminiscences of his childhood in Kent or his boyhood in and around Durham, and of his close observation of nature in either or both of these vicinities, in fact 'nature' in Smart's poetry occupies only such space as the waving lines of his intricate syntax and demanding metric allow to it. As J. B. Broadbent remarked thirty years ago, 'Smart's range of actual experience was narrow: he took most of his materials from books. They prompted him with detail for insights he already had to utter, so they do not construct pastiche. But the nature of

---

[11] Harriet Guest, *A Form of Sound Words. The Religious Poetry of Christopher Smart* (Oxford, 1989), p. 270.

[12] Smart's 'plod', however, is transitive. The *New English Dictionary* gives examples of this usage, of which the most obvious is Gray's 'The plowman homeward plods his weary way.' None of these underwrites the audacity of Smart's 'plods his task'. And yet the sense is clear; the beaver is industriously diligent. Is this rococo diction? It certainly isn't neo-classical.

[13] Joseph Burke, *English Art 1714–1800* (Oxford, 1976), 'The impact of the Rococo', p. 131.

his materials made him repetitive.' When Broadbent goes on to say, 'He has a series of favourite words such as *briny, scholar, pillar, churl, conscious*', this holds as true of *Hymns and Spiritual Songs* as of *Song to David*.[14] This does not make Smart any less of a poet; it makes of him only a poet not much interested in particularity and individuation, certainly not a landscape poet nor a 'nature-poet'. He was not, in Thomas Hardy's phrase, 'one who noticed such things'. And this brings him that much nearer to an artist like Francis Hayman.

Robert Brittain, whose pioneering studies in Smart have not been surpassed, remarked how distinctive in his lifetime was Smart's attitude to the Natural Creation:

The most important characteristic of Smart's nature material seems to me to be found in what one might call an essential happiness. In the period in which he wrote, such nature material as appears is almost universally handled in a mood of gentle melancholy or in a way which reveals a basic distrust. The great exception to this statement is of course Thomson, but even his work reveals these qualities at times. There are traces of them in Smart's early work ... but they are entirely lacking from his mature poems. Nowhere does that work show the slightest sense of nature as an alien and hostile power. On the contrary,

> Gentle nature seems to love us
> In each fair and finished scene,
> All is beauteous blue above us,
> All beneath is cheerful green.   (Hymn XIX, 4)

'Romantic shade', beloved of the late eighteenth century, is completely absent from the landscapes of Smart's mature work. There is never any gloom; there are no mists on the hills, no dark and threatening clouds in the sky. Not for him the 'dim religious light' of the graveyard school.[15]

It is indeed remarkable that Smart in his last years, penurious and derided, deprived of wife and children, writing against the clock to keep his creditors at bay, should have been able, not just in Hymn XIX but generally, to maintain this sunny assurance. And those religiously minded readers cannot be gainsaid who see here how a fervent faith can sustain an individual through the worst of worldly privations. All the same, it must be noticed that the ideology of rococo prescribed just such steady elation. In accord with that, Kenneth Clark entitled his chapter on rococo, 'The Pursuit of Happiness'. Smart's *Hymns and Spiritual Songs*,

[14] J. B. Broadbent (ed.), *A Song to David* (Rampant Lions Press, Cambridge, 1960), Introduction.

[15] Robert Brittain (ed.), *Poems by Christopher Smart* (Princeton, 1950), Introduction, p. 64.

no less than his *Song to David*, present that happiness not as pursued but as *secured* – under the only dispensation that provides such security, that is to say, redemption through Christ.

Rococo was, says Clark,[16] 'provocatively secular'. And certainly it seems so, in both Hogarth and Hayman. Yet Clark has no sooner delivered this verdict than he is forced to withdraw it, because of rococo churches in South Germany and Austria. Peter and Linda Murray make the same concession, speaking of these buildings as 'absurdly beautiful' – a judgement delivered from such an altitude of infidel connoisseurship as few of us can aspire to. Clark writes of the Zimmermans' pilgrimage church, Die Wieskirche in southern Bavaria:

enter it and the most incredible richness appears before your eyes. Heaven on earth. It is true that people entering the Gothic cathedrals left behind their life of material cares and seemed to pass into a different world. But it was a mysterious, awe-inspiring world in which hope of salvation was mixed with fear of death and judgement, and in simple communities the chief accent was on fear. Over the chancel arch in all parish churches was a scarifying representation of the Last Judgement, known as a Doom. In these Rococo churches the faithful are persuaded not by fear but by joy. To enter them is a foretaste of paradise.[17]

Smart of course never visited these buildings, nor could he have known of them. But we may legitimately summon them to mind, as the sort of church in which, by massed choirs, Smart's *Hymns and Spiritual Songs* might have been sung. There were doctrinal as well as aesthetic and social reasons why such churches could never have been built in England. But they are the logical end of sacralizing the rococo. One recalls Roy Strong's description of rococo as 'a style ideally suited to the architecture of transitory pleasures, to gardens, mascarades and theatre'. Smart seems to have envisaged and experienced the Christian life as a stroll – enraptured, of course – through infinitely extended, infinitely various, pleasure-gardens. It was not a vision available to Charles Churchill or John Wilkes.

Nor was it vouchsafed to hymnodists before Smart, or after him. John Wesley, however, revisiting Westminster Abbey in 1764, warmed to a monument by Roubiliac: 'What heaps of unmeaning stone and marble. But there was one tomb which showed common sense; that beautiful figure of Mr. Nightingale endeavouring to screen his lovely wife from

[16] Kenneth Clark, *Civilisation. A Personal View* (1969), p. 231.
[17] Ibid., p. 238.

death. Here indeed the marble seems to speak, and the statues appear only not alive.'[18] Between rococo and evangelical Christianity there is not such a gulf as current opinion takes for granted; though Smart may be the only gifted English poet who built the bridge between them. And Wesley's commendation should be noted, for it is characteristic: Roubiliac's sculpture, he says, 'showed common sense'. Common sense, whether in its eighteenth-century sense or as given a different inflection in modern usage, is what has never yet been applauded in the author of *Song to David*, not even by his admirers. We ought to look at Smart's hymns, especially his hymns for children, to see if after all common sense isn't what we can credit him with.

[18] Wesley's *Journal* for 16 March 1764; quoted by David Bindman, *The Rococo in England. A Symposium*, ed. Charles Hind (Victoria and Albert Museum 1986), p. 140.

9

Smart's elegance

Among the startlingly few people who have attended to Smart's *Hymns and Spiritual Songs* (1765), none seems to have taken hold of what is, from several points of view, the most striking feature of this collection of thirty-five poems: its metrical variety. This inattention is not altogether surprising. Metre is little favoured nowadays as a way into any poetry at all, partly because readers skilled in other aspects of poetry know themselves unskilled – ignorant, in fact – about metre. And rather plainly this is connected with the fact that so much English-language poetry of the present century has been either unmetred or else metred very roughly and licentiously. However, because so many otherwise qualified readers cannot trust themselves to scan correctly, the niceties of scansion that Smart asks for cannot be merely pointed to, they have to be briefly demonstrated.

To begin, then ... Hymn I ('New Year') is written in trochaic tetrameter quatrains:

> Word of endless adoration,
> Christ, I to thy call appear;
> On my knees in meek prostration
> To begin a better year.

The *abab* rhyme is made more sumptuous in that the *a* rhymes are feminine, the *b* rhymes masculine; which means that the odd lines have eight syllables, the even lines have (more normally for trochaic tetrameter) seven.

Hymn II ('Circumcision') is in a six-line stanza consisting of two iambic trimeters followed by an iambic tetrameter, twice over:

> When Abraham was bless'd,
> And on his face profess'd
> The Saviour Christ hereafter born,
> 'Thou pilgrim and estrang'd,
> Thy name, said God, is chang'd,
> Thy lot secur'd from want and scorn.'

To the relatively many readers who know the *Song to David* but no other poem by Smart, this stanza may look familiar. But in fact, despite an identical rhyme scheme, this is not the six-line stanza of the *Song*, because here tetrameters come where the *Song* has trimeters, and trimeters for the *Song*'s tetrameters. Thus this stanza is the *Song* stanza's mirror-image.

Hymn III ('Epiphany') reproduces the trochaic tetrameter quatrains of Hymn I. Hymn IV however ('Conversion of Saint Paul') rocks back once again from the trochaic beat to the iambic, in tetrameter quatrains rhyming in couplets:

> Thro' him, the chief, begot by Nun,
> Controul'd the progress of the sun;
> The shadow too, through him, retir'd
> The ten degrees it had acquir'd.

And Hymn V ('King Charles the Martyr') reproduces this.

Hymn VI ('The Presentation of Christ in the Temple') is again iambic, but in a five-line stanza where rhyme and indentation fool us into thinking we see two trimeter lines, whereas there is only one (the second):

> Preserver of the church, thy spouse,
>   From sacrilege and wrong,
> To whom the myriads pay their vows,
> Give ear, and in my heart arouse
>   The spirit of a nobler song.

Hymn VII ('Ash Wednesday. First Day of Lent') is likewise iambic, in quatrains that once again deceive the eye, and also (thanks to the *abab* rhyme) the ear, into thinking the stanza is built on simple alternation between tetrameter and trimeter, whereas in fact it is asymmetrical and only the last line of each quatrain is a trimeter:

> O Charity! that couldst receive
>   The dying thief's repentant pray'r;
> And didst upon the cross relieve
>   Thy fellow-suff'rer there!

(We have been given reason to believe that masked asymmetries, such as we find here and in the preceding hymn, were characteristic of rococo procedures in the decorative arts.)

The trochaic measure returns in Hymn VIII ('St Matthias'), in quatrains on the pattern set by Hymns I and III. Hymn IX, however

('The Annunciation of the Blessed Virgin'), builds a six-line stanza
more elaborate than any before, elaborate especially (and taxing to
both ear and voice) because it is neither iambic nor trochaic but both.
The proportion between the two measures is exactly regulated. For the
stanza, rhyming throughout in couplets, consists of four iambic trimeters followed by two seven-syllable trochaic tetrameters:

> O Purity, thou test
> Of love amongst the blest,
> How excellent thou art,
> The Lord Jehovah's heart,
>   Whose sweet attributes embrace
>   Every virtue, praise and grace.

Here we may break off this analysis; to persist with it through the rest of
the sequence would be tiresome, though abundantly worthwhile. One
thing that has emerged, however, is the strong presence of the trochaic
beat. Too much has been made of the extent to which the iambic
measure was imposed on the English ear from 1660 onwards because of
the predominance of the iambic pentameter, alike in heroic couplets
and blank verse. Trisyllabic metres were always available for use – by
Byrom for one, seeking his jaunty effects. Still, remembering what Ben
Jonson for instance had achieved in trochaic measures, we must be
struck by how rarely that falling metre figures thereafter in our poetry
until first Charles Wesley, and after him Smart, revived it. Hymn IX
proceeds:

> Thou fair and good dispos'd,
> 'Midst glories undisclos'd,
> Inspire the notes to play
> Upon the virgin's day;
>   High above all females nam'd,
>   And by Gabriel's voice proclaim'd.
>
> Glad herald, ever sent
> Upon some blest event,
> But never sped to men
> On such a charge till then –
>   When his Saviour's feet he kiss'd,
>   To promulge his birth dismiss'd.
>
> Hail mystery! thou source
> Of nature's plainest course,
> How much this work transcends
> Thine usual means and ends –

> Wherefore call'd, we shall not spare
> Louder praise, and oft'ner pray'r.

But if the work be new,
So shou'd the song be too,
By every thought that's born
In freshness of the morn;
> Every flight of active wings,
> Every shift upon the strings.

To praise the mighty hand
By which the world was mann'd,
Which dealt to great and small
Their talents clear of all;
> Kind to kind by likeness linkt,
> Various all, and all distinct.

Praise him seraphic tone ·
Of instruments unknown,
High strains on golden wire,
Work'd by etherial fire;
> Blowing on unceasing chords,
> 'King of kings, and lord of lords'.

Praise Hannah, of the three
That sang in Mary's key;
With her that made her psalm
Beneath the bow'ring palm;
> With the dame – Bethulia's boast,
> Honour'd o'er th'Assyrian host.

Praise him faith, hope, and love
That tend Jehovah's dove;
By men from lust repriev'd,
As females best conceive'd;
> To remount the man and muse
> Far above all earthly views.

This is hardly a good poem. Both Smart and we have to pay dearly for the metrical and rhyming exigencies he has imposed on himself, so that there are many crabbed obscurities we shall not pause to wrestle with. But what seems clear enough is the progression from 'this work' in stanza three to, in the next stanza, 'But if the work be new, / So shou'd the song be too', picked up by 'instruments unknown' in stanza seven. The argument is: since the virgin birth was unprecedented as a work of

God, so must be any work of man which celebrates that miraculous event. Therefore, we may and should infer, the poet has fashioned for this occasion a stanza that is similarly without precedent. Moreover, if we leave Hymn IX and think of the collection as a whole, the virgin birth is not in a class of its own; for God is *never* bound by precedent in any of His works (how could He be?), and the poet who aims adequately to praise Him and His works must attain so far as possible the same condition. If so, when Smart refuses to settle into one or two metrical patterns for his hymns, this is not mere restlessness, still less is it a display of dexterity, still less again is it a device for keeping us, readers or singers, off-balance and on our toes; it is to emulate, so far as human capacities can, the God-like attribute of being, in a phrase beloved of Smart, 'ever new'.

Imperfect as it is, this poem thus brings into focus the qualities and emphases which make Smart unique among devotional poets in English. The God whom he hymns is pre-eminently, if not quite exclusively, God the Creator, rather than God the Judge or God the Redeemer. In this Smart never ceased to be what he was to begin with, a brilliant Cambridge intellectual acclaimed as such, who in his Seatonian prize poems grappled with 'the Newtonian concept of a mechanical universe'.[1] What Smart came to reject in the Newtonian image of the universe was that it posited a Creator who was bound by precedents, though they were precedents of His own devising. Smart perceived, perhaps sooner than anyone else, the false analogy embodied in the expression, 'scientific law'. What scientists call a law is only very precariously analogous to what jurists understand by 'law'. If the Creator is by definition omnipotent, He cannot be bound by law – no more in the scientists' than in the jurists' sense. He is *free*. And so what Smart came to adore was above all the Creator's bounty; that bounty which, whether or not He at all often chose to advertise the fact, could break through all laws, Mosaic or Newtonian. Some commentators think that Smart came to this perception painfully, so damaging as it was to the presumptions of human Reason; another reading of the evidence – including as main exhibits in that evidence the dancing and exultant metres he employed – is that it came to him on the contrary as a liberation.

The dance moves most lightly on trochaic feet, as in Hymn III:

---

[1] William B. Oder, 'Madness and Poetry: a Note on Collins, Cowper, and Smart', *Bulletin of the New York Academy of Medicine*, April 1970.

> From a heart serene and pleasant
>   'Midst unnumber'd ills I feel,
> I will meekly bring my present,
>   And with sacred verses kneel.
>
> Muse, through Christ the Word, inventive
>   Of the praise so greatly due;
> Heav'nly gratitude retentive
>   Of the beauties ever new,
>
> Fill my heart with genuine treasures,
>   Pour them out before his feet,
> High conceptions, mystic measures,
>   Springing strong and flowing sweet.

This is the hymn for Epiphany – January 6th, the twelfth day after Christmas when the three *magi*, bearing gifts, arrived at the stable in Bethlehem; and Smart has already made the point that instead of their frankincense and myrrh, what he will bring is his verses. For that gift to be 'costly' enough, his verses must be, if not as in Hymn IX unprecedented, at all events 'inventive'. The reason behind that necessity is 'Heav'nly gratitude retentive / Of the beauties ever new'; and that explains the seeming paradox by which we have in Smart a poet continually innovative yet not at all interested in being 'original'. He does not in the least wish to break with the canon of poetic procedures, classical and neo-classical, that he has inherited. Simply he wants, and thinks it his pious duty, to be as various and innovative as possible within that prescribed range – a range that his efforts show to have been less prescriptive and exclusive than people suppose. The gulf between Smart and Blake – too often too idly associated – is very wide; and Claude Rogers was right to declare Smart 'Augustan'.[2] For instance, 'Springing strong and flowing sweet' refers immediately and without any embarrassment to a neo-classical commonplace best known from Pope's couplet: 'and praise the Easie Vigor of a Line / Where Denham's Strength, and Waller's Sweetness join'. By the same token, no hymn by Smart is a simple spurt of ardent feeling. Each of them has an argument, and when we have difficulty with them it is because the argument is too devious or too complicated or is pursued too elliptically. In this Epiphany hymn for instance the argumentative parallel between the poet and one or other of the three kings is overlaid by another progression from the speaker to begin with elderly – 'a western Palmer', looking

---

[2] Claude Rogers, *Order from Confusion Sprung* (1985), pp. 372–80.

at sunset – to the speaker as a reconstituted child. Every one of these hymns, good and less good alike, is structured through and through, metrically and in every other way.

The question that cannot be postponed any longer is in what sense, if at all, these hymns by Smart can be thought congregational. We have no evidence that a congregation ever performed any of them; and Smart's name does not appear in John Julian's *Dictionary*. More to the point, his dedication to metrical variety and experiment is at the furthest extreme from other hymnodists' self-denying restriction to short measure, long measure and common measure. And yet no one can think that Smart's hymns (nor his Psalter either, for that matter) are intended, like the Countess of Pembroke's Psalter, for private devotions only; his metres and above all his rhymes, richly vociferous and unsubtle, plainly call for and even embody the tones of trumpet and cymbal. Just here, surely, is the clue – the *Hymns and Spiritual Songs* were meant for congregational use, but for a few certain congregations of a special kind, congregations that never in the event had the use of them. The congregations that Smart had in mind were the massed congregations of cathedrals on festive occasions, led by trained choirs backed by small or not so small orchestras. This suggestion was first made by Father Christopher Devlin in what is still the boldest and most imaginative attempt to write Smart's biography.[3] Devlin makes sense of Smart's later life by supposing, on not inconsiderable evidence, that the woman he married (who later committed him to a madhouse) was covertly a Roman Catholic, who persuaded him to let the daughters of the marriage be educated by and as Papists. Smart's guilt and rage on this account brought about – so Father Devlin's theory proposes – a fiercely anti-papist Anglicanism that set about trying to supplant, as the metropolitan cathedral of Christendom, St Peter's in Rome by St Paul's in London. Nothing else can so well explain the astonishing lines in Hymn XIII ('St Philip and St James'):

> Great to-day thy song and rapture
> In the choir of Christ and WREN...

And if this is so, we must say that Smart's hymns were congregational in their intention, though not in the event.

This is as good a place as any to take up the matter of Smart's alleged madness. Though the expert testimony eighteen years ago was that on

3 Christopher Devlin, *Poor Kit Smart* (1961).

the evidence we have Smart was never insane by the criteria of today,[4] yet his madness is still confidently taken for granted, for the compelling and disgraceful reason that ever since A. E. Housman, if not since Robert Browning, some people have had a vested interest in arguing that in the Age of Reason a poet, to be authentic, had to be out of his wits. Not Smart alone, but poetry generally and indeed human rationality, are defamed by this prejudice. The *Song to David*, and even the fragmentary *Rejoice in the Lamb*, are works of a man in control of himself, who knows what it is he is doing. And certainly this is true of the author of *Hymns and Spiritual Songs for the Feasts and Festivals of the Church of England*.

Smart's anti-Romanism is very explicit in Hymn XX ('St Peter') and Hymn XXV ('St Luke'). But for that matter, as early as the third stanza of Hymn X he had defended his Anglicanism on its other flank, against the nonconformists. Smart was pugnacious and militant, and this is not his most attractive side; the best hymn-writers both before and after him tried to avoid sectarian bias. Still, even the strident hymn for St Luke ends with a beautifully compact rephrasing of Matthew 10.16:

> Innocent as doves our hearts,
> But as serpents wise.

For Smart's hymns are insistently scriptural; and the best way to vindicate his unashamedly poetic diction is to compare his verses with the Scripture texts that he meant us to have in mind. A delightful instance is in Hymn VII:

> The words of vengeance threat the tree,
> And fix their axes to the helves –
> Pray therefore – pray for such as flee
> Their Saviour and themselves

where the scriptural text is Matthew 3.10 (if not Luke 3.9):

> And now also the axe is layd unto the root of the trees: therefore every tree which bringeth not forth good fruite, is hewen downe, and cast into the fire.

It is the rhyme of the technically exact word 'helves' with the commonplace 'themselves' that manages the transition within four lines from a very exalted to a very homely diction. Another striking example comes in Hymn II, where the justly beloved text about the lilies of the field

---

[4] Oder, 'Madness and Poetry'.

that 'toil not, neither do they spin' (Matthew 6.28–9, Luke 12.27)
becomes:

> Ye lilies of perfume
> That triumph o'er the loom.

Contrary to what Wordsworth and sundry Wordsworthians have suggested, eighteenth-century poetic diction did not necessarily tend to
diffusion and wasteful circumlocution; in the hands of a master like
Smart it promoted on the contrary remarkable conciseness. For Smart's
nine words say what took Matthew and the Authorized Version more
than forty:

> And why take ye thought for raiment? Consider the lilies of the field, how
> they grow: they toile not, neither doe they spinne.
> And yet I say unto you, that even Solomon in all his glory, was not arrayed
> like one of these.

To be sure, Smart can achieve this masterly compression only by
trusting his readers to recall the much more extended passage in
Scripture; but that is only to say that he draws on the traditional
resource of allusion to achieve economy. (As when Ezra Pound, in a
famous and exuberantly witty letter, saluted Eliot's densely allusive *The
Waste Land* as 'let us say the longest poem in the English langwidge'.)

How far attention to metre can take us appears if we note that,
whereas it was the trochaic measure that supplied Smart with what are
by fairly common consent the masterpieces among *Hymns and Sacred
Songs* (Hymn XIII and the incomparable Nativity hymn, XXXII),
trochaic metre appears hardly at all in his later *Hymns for the Amusement
of Children* (1770). What is telling is that in the latter collection the one
place where the trochee reasserts itself and holds firm is a hymn about
gratitude for God's bounties, and the duties that imposes on one who
would bring Him offerings of *art*. It is called indeed 'Gratitude':

> I upon the first creation
>   Clap'd my wings with loud applause,
> Cherub of the highest station,
>   Praising, blessing, without pause.
>
> I in Eden's bloomy bowers
>   Was the heav'nly gardner's pride,
> Sweet of sweets, and flow'r of flowers,
>   With the scented tinctures dy'd.

Hear, ye little children, hear me,
 I am God's delightful voice:
They who sweetly still revere me,
 Still shall make the wisest choice.

Hear me not like Adam trembling,
 When I walk'd in Eden's grove;
And the host of heav'n assembling
 From the spot the traitor drove.

Hear me rather as the lover
 Of mankind, restor'd and free;
By the word ye shall recover
 More than that ye lost by Me.

I'm the Phoenix of the singers
 That in upper Eden dwell;
Hearing me Euphrates lingers,
 As my wondrous tale I tell.

'Tis the story of the Graces,
 Mercies without end or sum;
And the sketches and the traces
 Of ten thousand more to come.

Lift, my children, lift within you,
 Dread not ye the tempter's rod;
Christ our gratitude shall win you,
 Wean'd from earth, and led to God.

The rhetorical register is changed. Though we may well be aghast at the demands that Smart makes of the child that shall read this hymn, or hear it read, still he has made a determined effort to purge his style of its rococo fineries. Not of its airs and graces, however, certainly not of its graces. There is room for a distinct study of how 'grace', upper-case and lower-case, figures in Smart's writings. It would not be easy, because in Smart's day capitalization was often at the whim of the printer; and in any case he cherished and exploited the ambiguity between upper-case Grace, crucial in Christian theology, and lower-case 'grace', to be valued, says Thomas Bulfinch,[5] in 'all social enjoyments and elegant arts'. Between these two meanings or concepts, the essential bridge for Smart is another upper-case usage, the *Gratiae* (or *Charites*) of the ancients, three female beings (though Homer recognized only two) of

5 Thomas Bulfinch, *The Age of Fable* (1855).

whom Lemprière says: 'They presided over kindness, and all good offices, and their worship was the same as that of the nine Muses, with whom they had a temple in common.' Sir William Smith's *Classical Dictionary* is still more emphatic and specific about the importance of the Graces for artistry: 'Poetry, however, is the art which is especially favoured by them; and hence they are friends of the Muses, with whom they live together in Olympus.'[6] These are the Graces of 'Gratitude', Hymn XXII of *Hymns for the Amusement of Children*, and indeed, it might be argued, they are the presiding presences over the whole of that little regarded collection. For these thirty-three hymns at some points instruct children in seemly and decorous behaviour, at other times in central tenets of Christian ethics; and we shall think that the one concern sorts ill with the other, unless we recognize that the classical concept of the Graces binds the two together, thus throwing a bridge not just from the pagan world to the Christian, but also from social life to the life of art. Smart in 'Gratitude' is thus explaining to children what in Hymn IX of *Hymns and Spiritual songs* he had, much less successfully, explained to their parents: that the 'graces' of the poetic art – for instance, the niceties of prosody – are not in the least to be put by when the poet addresses a sacred theme, but on the contrary on such themes are to be displayed and exercised with a special virtuosity. For such virtuosity is the nearest human equivalent to the divine splendour, the divine *glory*. That Smart should want to make this point to children as well as to grown-ups shows, surely, how much it mattered to him. And the insistence shows that, even if Smart had not entertained unrealistic hopes of hearing his hymns sung in St Paul's Cathedral, still he was set on a course that diverged very widely from that of the other great hymnodists, such as Watts. In his view his art was not to be purged and castigated before it could address sacred matters, on the contrary those glorious matters should screw the poet up to realize the potentialities of his art as secular topics could not.

I have suggested that this divergence came about because, whereas Watts was chiefly concerned with the Divine Judge and the Divine Redeemer, Smart was hymning the Divine Creator. But what is specially poignant about the children's hymn, 'Gratitude', is that Smart is here concerned with the Redeemer as much as with the Creator. The poem seems to say that gratitude to God, which became impossible or sadly difficult at the fall of the First Adam in The Garden, has become

[6] *Everyman's Smaller Classical Dictionary* (1910; edn of 1952), p. 80.

possible again for the Second Adam; that is, for a mankind whose relations with God have been renewed by Christ's sacrifice. At the breaking of the first covenant, grateful adoration became obscured and obstructed by remorse; under the second covenant, that of Christ, it becomes again not a duty (for that it had always been) but a duty it is possible to perform. Hence the beautifully apt image of the phoenix, the bird reborn from its own ashes. (And yet the beauty is not *all* in the aptness, as distrustful puritans want it to be; there is a surplus, as Smart is at pains to insist.)

The childrens' hymns are bound together as a sequence in a way that has yet to be explored. So 'Gratitude' follows a hymn called 'Generosity' which ends by imputing gratitude to the Godhead. How this can be taxes the most devout imagination, and calls for more theology than most of us can manage. The best gloss I can come up with is that Christ, by embracing His tragic destiny, showed Himself grateful for it; or else, still more abstrusely, that when the Creator looked on His Creation and found it good, He was grateful for having had the chance to create it. Yet to what or whom can God be grateful? And how can Jesus, in so far as He is God, be thought to have any destiny at all? So difficult are the concepts brought into play by these seemingly more limpid and artless hymns that Smart wrote for children.

As we have seen, many of these hymns offer themselves as *definitions*. And others of them besides 'Gratitude' can be read as self-reflexive, as meditations by Smart on what he did when he was moved to write. One such is Hymn XIII, 'Elegance':

> 'Tis in the spirit that attire,
> Th' investiture of saints in heav'n;
> Those robes of intellectual fire,
> Which to the great elect are giv'n.

> 'Bring out to my returning son
> The robes for elegance the best';
> Thus in the height it shall be done,
> And thus the penitent be blest.

> 'Tis in the body, that sweet mien
> Ingenuous Christians all possess.
> Grace, easy motions, smiles serene,
> Clean hands and seemliness of dress.

> Whoever has thy charming pow'rs
> Is amiable as Kidron's swan,

> Like holy Esdras feeds on flow'rs,
>> And lives on honey like St. John.

Elegance in common usage includes gracefulness, and so there is a clear connection between this hymn and 'Gratitude', a connection signalled indeed by the word 'grace'. The *New English Dictionary* tells us: 'In early Latin *elegans* was a term of reproach, "dainty, fastidious, foppish", but in classical times it expressed the notions of refined luxury, graceful propriety, which are reproduced in the modern English use.' But it may be doubted whether the modern English use is any longer what the *New English Dictionary* confidently supposed. Current usage has overtones of the finical and foppish, representing a slide back towards early Latin *elegans*. To call a poem or even a person's deportment 'elegant' is nowadays less than fulsome praise. Smart on the other hand is solidly Augustan; his *elegans* is that of 'classical times'. And indeed it is not easy to find another English author who rates elegance so highly as to call it 'th' investiture of saints in heav'n'. This goes beyond what he had claimed for it in *Hymns and Spiritual Songs* II, where moreover he had applied it narrowly to verbal artistry:

> Let elegance, the flow'r
> Of words, in tune and pow'r,
>> Find some device of cleanest choice ...

In the childrens' hymn it is nowhere applied to *verbal* behaviour, but as we have seen with the overlapping term 'grace', it is of crucial importance to Smart that verbal behaviour, for instance in poems, be seen as only a special case of behaviour in general. His directions for bodily deportment – that it be sweet, graceful and easy, serene and seemly and clean – apply equally to the deportment that the poet wills upon the words in a poem. That is why, when we praise his 'phoenix' as beautifully apt ('I'm the phoenix of the singers / That in upper Eden dwell'), we must immediately add that the beauty is not all in the aptness – for that would be to scant the metrical grace, for instance. Elegance is thus for Smart not a kind or component of beauty, but a principle that is ampler than beauty at the same time as it is more precise. Only if it is given that ample sense can we without absurdity find in its wardrobe 'robes of intellectual fire'. And we can admire the elegance of closing the poem with three scriptural allusions, before we have tracked down the allusions to see if they are apt. We may go so far as to wonder whether elegance in this strenuous sense, as more comprehensive than 'beauty' though comprehending that, does not give us the clue to the otherwise elusive aesthetic of the rococo. To do so would install the rococo as eminently commonsensical.

10

The author of 'Amazing Grace'

In 1836 Edward Fitzgerald, who would go on to write *The Rubaiyat of Omar Khayyam*, wrote to a correspondent: 'I have just read Southey's Life of Cowper; that is to say, the first Volume. It is not a book to be read by every man at the fall of the leaf. It is a fearful book. Have you read it? Southey hits hard at Newton in the dark; which will give offence to many people: but I perfectly agree with him. At the same time, I think that Newton was a man of great power ...'[1] The Newton in question is not the great Sir Isaac, but the Reverend John Newton (1725–1807), author of 'Glorious things of thee are spoken' and 'How sweet the Name of Jesus sounds', as well as of 'Amazing grace! (how sweet the sound!)', which last must surely be the best-known and most-loved hymn in North America – not just among church-goers either.

What Fitzgerald means by 'Southey hits hard at Newton in the dark', is the very heavy implication in Robert Southey's book that Newton exerted a malign influence on the gentleman-poet William Cowper, when the latter was among his parishioners in Buckinghamshire. The relationship was certainly very close, as we see from Newton's and Cowper's collaboration on *Olney Hymns* (1779). By that time Newton had put behind him nearly fifty years of exceptionally lurid experience. Sent to sea as an eleven-year-old boy, Newton testified that soon thereafter he felt at home in 'settled infidelity', provoked or precipitated (so he claimed) by a reading of the philosopher Shaftesbury. Newton was later flogged as a deserter from the Royal Navy. Thereafter he spent fifteen months ashore, half-starved and ill-treated, under a slave-dealer in West Africa. Between the ages of twenty-three and twenty-nine he captained a slave-ship; and from 1755 to 1764 he was chiefly in Liverpool, consorting with the Wesley brothers, with George

---

[1] *Letters and Literary Remains of Edward Fitzgerald*, edited by William Aldis Wright (1889), vol. I, p. 34.

Whitefield and with nonconformist ministers. It was in 1764 that Newton was appointed, not without difficulty, to the curacy of Olney.

Fitzgerald and Southey knew of Newton's turbulent youthful adventures in the seamy underworld of Georgian society. And so did Cowper. Newton was at pains to see that they did. For whereas in one sense it is true that Newton the priest had put his past behind him, in another sense he brought it with him, for it was his stock in trade. He told and retold the story of how he had come to his ministry, as testimony to how Christ's saving Grace could descend on the most reprobate sinners. Before him John Bunyan, and since him many evangelists to the present day, have thus borne witness. And so it is no surprise that one modern retelling of the story – *Amazing Grace: John Newton's Story*, by John Pollock (1981) – should come before us with a special commendation from the Reverend Billy Graham. Equally the High Churchman Southey has not been the last to protest that such strong meat can be too much for delicate stomachs like that of the melancholiac Cowper; that such necessarily 'Charismatic' preaching can have on such precariously balanced souls the opposite effect from what was intended, driving them further into the abysses of terror and despair from which they need to be rescued. It needs to be said, however, that, as regards the Newton–Cowper relationship, the evidence can be read in quite another way, to vindicate Newton, as Cowper himself would have vindicated him.

In any case, this is only one of the charges which cultivated or would-be cultivated persons level at the sort of evangelical Christianity that John Newton professed and embodied. People who have not read the angry late-Victorian recriminations of Samuel Butler or Augustus Hare, not to speak of earlier corrosive pages by Dickens, have all the same got the message: evangelicalism, influential through all the protestant denominations, perfected (so it is said) a formulaic rigmarole for the benefit of that bogey-figure, the Victorian paterfamilias. The evangelical idiom supplied the Victorian papa (or his surrogate – the uncle, the guardian) with a screen to mask from others, and perhaps from himself, his own domineering, his hypocrisy, his lack of feeling. So goes the indictment.

However that may be, the idiom was not a Victorian but an eighteenth-century invention:

Yes, Madam, the Lord has done great things for us since we came home. He sent a chariot of love for dear Eliza. We almost saw her mount. Surely she was in Heaven, and Heaven in her, before she left the earth. The manner of her dismission had a merciful effect upon us, so that, though it was in one view like pulling off a limb, yet upon the whole we felt that praises were much more suitable for us than complaints. I still weep for her more or less every day, but I thank the Lord I have not dropped one tear of sorrow. My Dear likewise has been wonderfully supported.

These reflections on the death of a fifteen-year-old were written in 1785, though not published until 1824, in *The Aged Pilgrim's Triumph over Sin and the Grave*, a posthumous collection of Newton's letters.

It is obvious why unbelievers find such a passage pernicious and abhorrent, nor will they be mollified (from their standpoint they should not be) if we oblige them to concede that only a strong intelligence could have framed the surprising progression, 'I still weep ... but ... have not dropped one tear ...' Much less comfortable is the situation of the professing Christian who finds his or her teeth set on edge. If for instance we object that such writing is 'unctuous', we may properly be reminded that only recently did 'unctuous' lose its connection with the sacrament of Unction, so as to become a derogatory term. And yet even in its own day such writing set teeth on edge. John Newton was still alive when the maverick nonconformist John Foster (1770–1843) published in 1805 an essay which attracted much attention, 'On some of the Causes by which Evangelical Religion has been rendered less acceptable to Persons of cultivated Taste'. Foster's *Essays* were reviewed, carefully and cordially, by Robert Hall (1764–1831), a prominent pulpit-orator for the Baptists, whose idiom was not evangelical at all but far more glittering and tumid, a sort of sub-Johnsonese which was much admired in Hall's lifetime. Hall demurs only a little, though at times perceptively, at Foster's argument that the evangelical idiom was in effect a *jargon*. (See, for a similar objection, Coleridge in his *Table Talk* in 1827.) But towards the end of his review Hall expressed one important reservation:

On the whole, let it once for all be remembered, that men of taste form a very small part of the community, of no greater consequence in the eyes of their Creator than others; that the end of all religious discourse is the salvation of souls; and that to a mind which justly estimates the weight of eternal things, it will appear a greater honour to have converted a sinner from the error of his way, than to have wielded the thunder of a Demosthenes, or to have kindled the flame of a Cicero.[2]

---

[2] *Selected Works of the late Rev. Robert Hall, A.M.* (1839), p. 257.

It is a pity Hall did not allow that there were women of taste, as well as men. But otherwise his warning certainly applies today. There is reason to believe that perhaps a numerical majority of professing and more or less fervent Christians today, of all races world wide, would find John Newton's arguments and even much of his vocabulary more agreeable and more comforting than the arguments and vocabulary of the late T. S. Eliot.

For after all, in the case of the worst afflictions – for instance, the least foreseeable bereavements – what arguments but John Newton's are available to the pastor of souls? Observing how many humble and god-fearing people still help to finance the degrading antics of television evangelists, we can only answer, 'None'. At the same time as such manifestations make us want more than ever to keep our distance from the evangelical idiom, or from its excesses, they must remind us that we do so at our peril.

There are those who, while still uncomfortable with the idiom of *The Aged Pilgrim's Triumph*, do not want to give up the pleasure of singing in a congregation, 'Glorious things of thee are spoken'. And it is open to them to propose that the exigencies of verse pruned away from Newton's English the unctuous or mawkish or formulaic idiosyncrasies that disfigure his prose. This argument is ingenious and appealing, but ultimately it will not hold water:

> Who can faint while such a river
>   Ever flows their thirst to assuage –
> Grace, which, like the Lord the giver,
>   Never fails from age to age.
>
> Blest inhabitants of Zion,
>   Washed in the Redeemer's blood;
> Jesus, whom their souls rely on,
>   Makes them kings and priests to God.

The rhyme 'Zion'/'rely on', though in singing we belt it out with a will and a special sort of relish, comes at us off the page as almost comically outrageous – such a desperate expedient as it is, yet proffered so unashamedly. What we relish in it is a sort of *naiveté*, such as we can learn to savour in *The Aged Pilgrim's Triumph* also:

You might well expect to hear from us before now; I should have let you know that the carpet came safe, which is all I have to say of it. How it looks, how it fits, and how much it is admired, I leave my dear to inform you; I suppose she will likewise thank you for your trouble.

Carpets and such fine things lie out of my department. The path through this wilderness to the Kingdom of Glory is not spread with carpets; if it were, shoes of iron and brass would be unnecessary, and if they were not needful, the Lord would not have provided them.

But he knows the way is rough, and provides accordingly.

This determination to improve every occasion is exasperating to some people, comically entertaining to others. But these latter play a dangerous game, if they find John Newton delightfully quaint. If our relish of him is in this way condescending, we fail to take the force of him when he strikes home:

> But, when I see Thee as Thou art,
> I'll praise Thee as I ought.

The tautness of such an expression does not come by inspired accident to a man too naïve to ask himself if he is sincere. John Newton, the bluff and forthright sailorman – it is not an altogether false portrait, but it is a self-portrait painted for a purpose. Therefore it is at least partly a *persona* for public consumption, though designed to serve very worthy ends like the saving of souls and the abolition of the slave-trade. Newton's simplicity and artlessness are partly authentic, partly assumed; and only sometimes can we afford to take them at face value.

Consider the hymn that Lord David Cecil dug out for *The Oxford Book of Christian Verse* in 1940:

> In evil long I took delight,
>   Unawed by shame or fear,
> Till a new object struck my sight,
>   And stopp'd my wild career:
> I saw One hanging on a Tree
>   In agonies and blood,
> Who fix'd His languid eyes on me,
>   As near His Cross I stood.
>
> Sure never till my latest breath
>   Can I forget that look:
> It seem'd to charge me with His death,
>   Though not a word He spoke;
> My conscience felt and own'd the guilt,
>   And plunged me in despair;
> I saw my sins His Blood had spilt,
>   And help'd to nail Him there.

Alas! I knew not what I did!
    But now my tears are vain:
Where shall my trembling soul be hid?
    For I the Lord have slain!
– A second look He gave, which said
    'I freely all forgive;
This blood is for thy ransom paid;
    I die, that thou may'st live.'

Thus, while His death my sin displays
    In all its blackest hue,
Such is the mystery of grace,
    It seals my pardon too.,
With pleasing grief, and mournful joy,
    My spirit now is fill'd,
That I should such a life destroy, –
    Yet live by Him I kill'd!

This is a moving poem admirably bold and clear, and certainly evangelical. One imagines it sung with a will in any congregation of the 'born again'. Yet 'pleasing grief, and mournful joy' is not a forthright expression, and the emotional state that it describes may be thought enervated, even luxurious. This makes Newton's poem almost modish; certainly it reveals it as very much of its period, which literary history has called the Age of Sensibility. The text that is always cited to define this is Henry Mackenzie's *The Man of Feeling* (1771), though Mackenzie should not be made to carry a blame that ought to be shared more widely. This is to assume that the phenomenon is blameable, and most commentators have thought that it is, to the point where some of them have not scrupled to call it 'decadent'. Its characteristic interest in complicated and ambiguous, even oxymoronic states of sentiment – grief crossed with pleasure, mournfulness with joy – have been thought to evince an enjoyment of feeling 'for its own sake', a sort of connoisseurship that contrives, to stimulate a jaded palate, ever spicier concoctions of feelings such as a sounder taste supposes distinct, even mutually exclusive. We may say in Newton's defence that at least the *occasion* of the oxymorons – the Crucifixion of the Redeemer – is abundantly clear and momentous. But it may still be felt that we are invited to dwell on the emotional compound, to luxuriate in it. Another way of explaining our discomfort is to ask whether, when the believer contemplates the Crucifixion, he does not experience a painful oscillation or alternation of feelings rather than an instant compounding of them. At least the case seems to show that, whereas evangelicalism is often thought a by-blow of the Romantic Movement, its affinities initially were rather with an earlier and more dubious movement of secular taste. And Newton, though he sometimes chose to pretend that he was a 'primitive', a sort of Grandma Moses, was not unaffected by such a shift of taste. We may wonder whether even today Evangelicals are not to be numbered among the remote progeny of Henry Mackenzie.

To wonder so it is not necessarily to sneer. By thus accommodating the truths of the Gospel to an established secular taste, Newton was perhaps doing again in a later generation what Johnson in his *Lives of the Poets* had by implication applauded Isaac Watts for having done: bringing sectarian minds back into contact with the mainstream of English culture. Just as we fail to esteem Watts' cultural achievement if we do not notice the ferocity of his Dissenting rivals such as Thomas Bradbury, so we fail to salute Newton's achievement if we are ignorant of the obscurantist ferocity that characterized Anglican evangelicalism under George III.

There was for instance Augustus Montague Toplady (1740–75) who, himself a renegade Wesleyan, assailed John Wesley with extraordinary vituperative venom (for instance, in 1772, 'The satanic guilt . . . is only equalled by the satanic shamelessness.') Toplady's 'Rock of Ages, cleft for me' – in *A Collection of Hymns*, 1776 – is immovable from its place in English hymnody, having attained what may once have seemed the supreme accolade of being put into Latin by William Ewart Gladstone in 1839. But alas, it is the work of a scurrilous bigot. Or there is William Romaine (1714–95). Romaine, son of a Huguenot immigrant who fled France after the revocation of the Edict of Nantes, graduated from Oxford in 1734, just too soon to experience the influence of the Wesley brothers in the university. He was ordained in 1736. In 1753 he wrote a pamphlet against a bill in parliament for naturalizing the Jews. By this time he was an ardent adherent of the Calvinistic Methodism of George Whitefield, which had set Whitefield on a collision course with the Wesleys. Romaine was compelled, among scenes of turmoil and public tumult, to resign his lectureship at St George's, Hanover Square, in London. His old university denied him the pulpit of the University Church after two sermons that he preached there in 1757 on justification by faith not works. In 1764, after further disputes, he was installed in another London church, St Anne's, Blackfriars, where he is said to have ministered to 500 communicants on his first Good Friday. Newton who, after he became in 1780 rector of St Mary Woolnoth, was the only evangelical clergyman in London apart from Romaine, seems to have maintained civil relations with Romaine, but confessed in private that he thought his ministrations often harmful. If there are still people who envisage Hanoverian London (or Oxford, Bath or Chelten-ham) in terms of sedan-chairs and elegant porcelain, religious torpor and suave scepticism in drawing-rooms, a look at influential men like Toplady and Romaine will disabuse them. And let it be noted that both of them were priests of the Established Church; we are not looking at dishevelled nonconformists in obscure conventicles. This was the company from which Newton had to distance himself, and he did so by making prudent overtures to secular literary taste.

His collaboration with Cowper on the *Olney Hymns* should be seen in this light; Newton was going out on a limb. Romaine had written, in his *Essay on Psalmody* (1775), of 'a temptation, into which most of our hymn-singers have fallen:

I have heard several of them, who would by no means be thought common rate understandings, object to Sternhold and Hopkins. They wonder I would make use of this version which they think is poor flat stuff, the poetry is miserable, and the language low and base. To which I answer: They had a scrupulous regard for the very words of scripture, and to those they adhered closely and strictly: so much so as to render the versification not equal to Mr. Pope. I grant, it is not always smooth: It is only here and there brilliant. But what is a thousand times more valuable, It is generally the sentiment of the holy Spirit. That is very rarely lost. And this should silence every objection – *It is the word of God*. Moreover the version comes nearer to the original, than any I have ever seen, except the Scotch, which I have made use of, when it appeared to me better expressed than the English. You may find fault with the manner of ekeing out a verse for the sake of rhyme; but what of that? Here is every thing great, and noble, and divine, although not in Dr. Watts' way or stile. It is not, like his, fine sound and florid verse; as good old Mr. Hall used to call it, *Watts jingle*. I do not match those psalms with what is now admired in poetry; although time was, when no less a man than the Rev. T. Bradbury in his sober judgment thought so meanly of Watts hymns as commonly to term them *Watts whyms*. And indeed compared to the scripture they are like a little taper to the sum: As for his psalms they are so far from the mind of the Spirit, that I am sure if David was to read them, he would not know any one of them to be his.

Besides you are offended at the Scripture style, and Dr. Watts must mend it. This is owing to a very false taste. For the scripture wants no mending; nay it is always worse for mending. It is plain in majesty. God has not written it to please the imagination, but to convert the heart, and to comfort and to edify the soul.

Though we have too much reason to convict the dissenting sects, in the last century and in this, of literary as well as architectural philistinism, a passage like this shows them anticipated and outdone by an Anglican. Isaac Watts of course had been a Dissenter. And sure enough Romaine, we are told, 'was strongly opposed to dissenters, holding the Calvinist side of the articles as the essence of the Church of England'.

Newton called himself a Calvinist, but not a *high* Calvinist. The Calvinism of Toplady, Romaine and Whitefield was 'high' in more ways than one, including the sense of 'high society'. Though Newton had his high-born patrons, notably the 2nd Earl of Dartmouth (William Legge, 1731–1801, called 'the Psalm-singer'), George Whitefield's lack of the organizing abilities that so distinguished and engrossed John Wesley made Whitefield hand over the organization of the Calvinist Methodists to his noble convert, the Countess of Huntingdon, who shrewdly enough made a point of cultivating the high-born and influential. Newton was happier with the lower orders, as Wesley was also.

Newton's association with the Wesleys in Liverpool in the 1750s left its mark on him as a poet, despite the Wesleys' fierce anti-Calvinism. One source for 'Amazing Grace', for instance, is surely Charles Wesley's early 'Free Grace' (1739), of which the first stanza reads:

> And can it be, that I should gain
>   An In'trest in the Saviour's Blood!
> Dy'd He for Me? – who caus'd his Pain!
>   For Me? – who Him to Death pursu'd.
> Amazing Love! how can it be
> That Thou, my GOD, shouldst die for Me?

'Amazing Grace' goes as follows:

> Amazing grace! (how sweet the sound!)
>   That sav'd a wretch like me!
> I once was lost, but now am found,
>   Was blind, but now I see.
>
> 'Twas grace that taught my heart to fear,
>   And grace my fears reliev'd;
> How precious did that grace appear,
>   The hour I first believ'd.
>
> Through many dangers, toils, and snares,
>   I have already come;
> 'Tis grace has brought me safe thus far,
>   And grace will lead me home.

> The Lord has promis'd good to me,
>   His word my hope secures;
> He will my shield and portion be,
>   As long as life endures.
>
> Yea, when this heart and flesh shall fail,
>   And mortal life shall cease;
> I shall possess, within the vail,
>   A life of joy and peace.
>
> The earth shall soon dissolve like snow,
>   The sun forbear to shine;
> But God, who call'd me here below,
>   Will be for ever mine.

This is the text as printed and discussed by Madeleine Forell Marshall and Janet Todd in their *English Congregational Hymns in the Eighteenth Century* (Lexington, Kentucky, 1982). However, I have seen other versions where the last quatrain reads:

> When we've been there ten thousand years,
>   Bright shining as the sun,
> We've no less days to sing God's praise
>   Than when we've first begun.

This is much more naïve. It is also plainly wrong, misconceived; for Eternity is not time going on for ever, but a different dimension altogether, from which the totting up of numbers ('ten thousand years') is accordingly the worst distraction. But in either version Newton's poem is surely superior to Wesley's, which in its penultimate stanza declares:

> Still the small inward Voice I hear,
>   That whispers all my Sins forgiv'n;
> Still the atoning Blood is near,
>   That quench'd the Wrath of hostile Heav'n.

'Hostile Heaven'? The sentiment is surely heretical, if not blasphemous; at all events, drastically unconsidered. (So is 'ten thousand years', though less damagingly.) Will it be said that these are theological, not literary, objections? But just here is the difficulty in trying to take literary account of religious poetry. Of course, if you believe that theology is so much mumbo-jumbo anyway, then the difficulty disappears (though so do the poems, except as antiquarian relics). But if one believes that theology is an intricately structured intellectual edifice (as historically we must acknowledge it to be, even if we think its initial postulates untenable), then a poet's sloppiness in handling the concepts he offers to deal with has to count against him. For those concepts appear in his text as *words*; and an unconsidered use of *words* has always been thought, in poetry, a fault.

Madeleine Forell Marshall and Janet Todd praise the language of 'Amazing Grace' as 'transparent'. And of course we see what they mean. But as they doubtless recognize, 'transparent' is a cop-out: in effect a confession by the critic that he or she is defeated. We can exert ourselves, calling on historical scholarship, to uncover in the text some of those inspissations which are meat and drink to criticism, which this poet so provokingly denies us. 'Vail', we may discover or recall, is not an alternative spelling for 'veil', but refers to (*Oxford English Dictionary*) 'the piece of precious cloth separating the sanctuary from the body of the temple or the tabernacle'; and Newton's use of it is scriptural, in the Epistle to the Hebrews (6.19–20):

> Which hope we have as an anchor of the soul, both sure and stedfast, and which entereth into that within the vail;
> Whither the forerunner is for us entered, even Jesus, made an high priest for ever after in the order of Melchisedec.

And it certainly helps the resonance of 'amazing', in both Wesley and Newton, if we let the *Dictionary* instruct us that 'amazement' had the meaning of 'panic' in 1706, and of 'stupefaction, frenzy' in 1746. But these are, if not quite pedantries, no disproof of Marshall's and Todd's honest perception that Newton's language here soars free of all the nets that critic-fowlers may set for it. (If deconstructionists must maintain that such 'transparency' is linguistically impossible, that is their problem.)

A lot of Newton's hymns are disarming in this way, though seldom to quite this extent. We have to resist so far as we can being disarmed, not for the sake of the dignity of the critic's function (which is a matter of very little moment), but because in this as in any other body of poetry we are aware that some pieces are better than others, and the awareness calls out to be articulated. One instrument that lies ready to our hand, which however we seldom use, is *metre*. For another of Charles Wesley's bequests to John Newton, of the greatest importance, was Wesley's demonstration that the supposedly 'vulgar' trisyllabic metres, thought the appropriate vehicle only for 'light verse', could be pressed into the service of sacred verse. A remarkable number of Newton's best hymns

dance in tripping anapaests. A particularly charming example is
'Green Fields':

> How tedious and tasteless the hours
> When Jesus no longer I see.
> Sweet prospects, sweet birds and sweet flowers
> Have lost all their sweetness to me;
> The midsummer sunshines are dim,
> The fields strive in vain to look gay.
> But when I am happy in Him,
> December's as pleasant as May.
>
> His name yields the sweetest perfume,
> And sweeter than music his voice;
> His presence disperses my gloom
> And makes all within me rejoice.
> I should, were he always thus nigh,
> Have nothing to wish nor to fear.
> No mortal as happy as I!
> My summer would last all the year.
>
> Content with beholding His face,
> My all to His pleasure resign'd,
> No changes of season or place
> Would make any change in my mind.
> For, bless'd with a sense of His love,
> A palace a toy would appear,
> And prisons would palaces prove
> If Jesus would dwell with me there.
>
> Dear Lord, if indeed I am Thine,
> If Thou art my sun and my song,
> Say, why do I languish and pine?
> And why are my winters so long?
> Oh drive these dark clouds from my sky;
> Thy soul-cheering presence restore.
> Or take me to Thee up on high
> Where winter and clouds are no more.

I have called this 'charming' – a slack and question-begging epithet,
usually or inevitably condescending, certainly no part of any responsible critical vocabulary. And yet in this case it is exact, surely. For it
belongs in the same register with all the epithets in the first stanza:
'tedious', 'tasteless', 'sweet' ... sweet ... sweet', 'dim', 'gay', 'happy',
'pleasant' – it is the very vocabulary of an indulged Hanoverian

heroine, like Sheridan's Lydia Languish. It is the language of the Age of Sensibility once again; and Newton deploys it so extravagantly, only so as to undermine and discredit it (not malevolently, however) in the rest of the hymn. It is only after worldly pleasures have turned out 'tedious and tasteless', that one can savour pleasure and sweetness that are not evanescent. The poet's focus is still on *pleasure*: if pleasure is what you aim at in life, then (he asserts) only the Gospel can give it to you in a fashion that won't go stale. Calvinism is often, unthinkingly, supposed to be a belief that cannot help but be morose, hag-ridden; but Newton's life as well as his poetry affirms that *his* Calvinism was on the contrary joyous, life-enhancing. Far more than his diction, his metre enforces this. To those who have heard 'Green Fields' rendered by that exceptional British quartet, The Wattersons[3], this will be self-evident: the elated *brio* of their performance brings out the joyousness. And we are indebted to the musicologists for telling us that, whereas the melody to which the Wattersons sing this hymn may originate in a Bach cantata, its immediate source seems to have been a parlour ballad, 'Both Sexes Give Ear to my Fancy'. Though it is well attested how often and how shrewdly the hymn-writers adopted secular and even bawdy melodies to their sacred purposes, Newton's practice along these lines seems to have been special: metres and melodies associated with erotic fulfilment have been taken over by him to embody spiritual fulfilment. Such crossings-over of erotic with religious ecstasy have been generally condemned; yet it may be objected that such condemnations depend on an unargued rating down of human sexuality.

Marshall and Todd are severe on that substantial body of Newton's hymns which may be called, as they call it, 'sermon-hymns'. Such hymns, they say, fall into three parts: 'the text (which may be a Bible story or a general truth or observation), an explanation of the relevance of the text to the lives of the singers, and then a prayer'. Newton, they say, 'sacrificed many hymns to this formula, which, in its lack of subtlety, is essentially prosaic as well as unsuitable for communal song'.

But we may contest this, in so far as it may be thought to bear on a hymn like this:

> The prophet's sons, in times of old,
>   Though to appearance poor,
> Were rich without possessing gold,
>   And honour'd though obscure.

---

[3] *Sound, Sound your Instruments of Joy* (Topic Records Limited, 1977).

> In peace their daily bread they eat,
>   By honest labour earn'd;
> While daily at Elisha's feet
>   They grace and wisdom learn'd.
>
> The prophet's presence cheer'd their toil,
>   They watch'd the words he spoke,
> Whether they turn'd the furrow'd soil,
>   Or fell'd the spreading oak.
>
> Once, as they listened to his theme,
>   Their conference was stopp'd;
> For one beneath the yielding stream
>   A borrow'd Axe had dropp'd.
>
> 'Alas! it was not mine.' he said,
>   'How shall I make it good?'
> Elisha heard, and when he pray'd,
>   The iron swam like wood.
>
> If God, in such a small affair,
>   A miracle performs,
> It shows his condescending care
>   Of poor unworthy worms.
>
> Though kings and nations in his view
>   Are but as motes and dust.
> His eye and ear are fix'd on you,
>   Who in his mercy trust.
>
> Not one concern of ours is small,
>   If we belong to him:
> To teach us this, the Lord of all
>   Once made the iron swim.

It may well be true that few pastors and few congregations nowadays can be brought to sing a hymn like this. But they may be the poorer for abjuring it – poorer spiritually, but culturally also. I have said that it is honesty, the refusal to slip anything over on the reader or the congregation, which pins down the miracle at its most literal, by *rhyme*:

> 'Alas, it was not mine', he said,
>   How shall I make it good?
> Elisha heard, and when he pray'd
>   The iron swam like wood.

And, I went on (in *Augustan Lyric*, 1974), 'it is the same wide-eyed concern to get the point home at its most astounding which justifies what seems at first sight a clear case of that bane of eighteenth-century poetry, the superfluous because "stock" epithet:

> For one beneath the yielding stream
> A borrow'd axe had dropp'd.

For it is of the nature of streams to "yield". This one didn't – and that's just the point; simple enough in all conscience, but in its very simplicity massively disconcerting.' Now, after fifteen years, the word I'm not sure about is 'wide-eyed'; for I've come to suspect that Newton is a more artful writer than I had supposed, and never more so than when he seems most artless. More certainly, I would now retract my comment on the poem: 'Its poetic virtues are minimal perhaps, yet real and rare.' If its virtues are minimal, they represent a minimum which few poets of the present day, whether secular or sacred, can attain to – and this not because today's writers are sloppy or incompetent (though of course many are), but because the tradition they immediately inherit is much less fine-tuned, a tradition in which for instance, since 'stock' epithets have been discountenanced, there is no possibility of reversing their import surprisingly.

The prejudice against such poems with their strong story line represents, one may suspect, a slopping over into sacred verse of a predilection which has long damaged our secular verse – for the lyrical effusion over other sorts of poem. Voices that are now raised in favour of narrative verse ought to speak up also for a firmly narrative poem like this. If they fail to do so, it is not because of aesthetic predilections but because John Newton's sort of Christianity, though manifestly alive and thriving to this day, is such as cultivated Christians refuse to countenance.

11

William Cowper and the plain style

Nearly forty years ago I pontificated: 'After Ben Jonson, Cowper is the most neglected of our poets.'[1] That aggrieved sentiment, which I do not disown though I am nowadays amused at my pompousness, has informed most considerations of Cowper since. Yet to little purpose; for Cowper, it seems safe to say, is still not accepted as a great poet, in the sense in which that laurel is readily bestowed on Donne or Hopkins, Coleridge or Wordsworth or Blake. And when he is grudgingly accorded something like that rank, it is not as a *lyric* poet – which is what we have to claim for him if we want to extol him as a writer of hymns.

In this situation, there is every temptation for Cowper enthusiasts to minimize or rule out the objections that can be, and have been, advanced against Cowper – not poetically indeed but (what is in any case inextricable from the poetry) religiously. Cowper, we would do well to acknowledge, had too many scruples, and gloried in having them. Southey, in his influential biography (1835), called on Coleridge's *Table Talk* to define the disposition which thus expressed itself: 'that mood of mind which exaggerates, and still more greatly mistakes, the inward depravation of man'. If we track this back to its origin in Coleridge, there is a sort of comedy; for it turns out that the definition is thrown out when Coleridge in 1830 is commending Southey's *Life of Bunyan*, at the same time reproving it for not noticing in Bunyan the same proclivity that is to be castigated in Cowper. However Southey, as nearly always commonsensical behind his orotundities, has a specific instance in mind which bears out his allegation. This is a passage from Cowper's autobiographical *Memoir* (1766–7) which deals with the public appointment that, once he had decided he could not face up to it, propelled him into the psychotic 'retirement' (a black adaptation of

---

[1] Donald Davie, 'The Critical Principles of William Cowper', *The Cambridge Journal*, VII (1953), pp. 182–8.

an Augustan commonplace) that was to be his mode of life thereafter.
At thirty-two, says Southey:

He began to be a little apprehensive of approaching want; and under that
apprehension, talking one day of his affairs with a friend, he expressed his hope
that if the clerk of the journals of the House of Lords should die, his kinsman
Major Cowper, who had the place in his disposal, would give him the appointment. 'We both agreed,' says he, 'that the business of the place being transacted
in private would exactly suit me; and both expressed an earnest wish for his
death, that I might be provided for. Thus did I covet what God had com-
manded me not to covet; and involved myself in still deeper guilt by doing it in
the spirit of a murderer . . .'

We may be shocked that offices of remuneration under the Crown
should be in the gift of privileged families like the Cowpers. But that is
not the source of what Cowper records as his discomfort, indeed
distress. Such was the accepted way of filling such offices. As Southey
says: 'when Cowper chose the law for his profession, both his father and
himself reckoned upon their family patronage as one reason for this
choice'. And accordingly, 'that the wish whereof he accuses himself
amounted to any thing more than what every one feels who looks for
promotion by seniority, or for any other advantage accruing upon the
decease of some person whose death would otherwise be to him a matter
of mere indifference, is what no one can believe'. And so Southey has
earned the right to be magisterial: 'Common nature is not so depraved
as to form murderous wishes for such motives.' Cowper's scrupulosity,
in this as in more important matters, was excessive and (one cannot
help feeling) self-aggrandizing. His sensibility was in this way morbid,
in a loose but thoroughly acceptable sense. He came to believe that he
was damned; but he was determined that damnation should be his
portion, and took even a twisted gratification from that conviction.
Before we can appreciate this poet, that wilful morbidity in him has to
be taken into account. It was not what his Calvinism committed him to
– as the sunny Calvinism of his collaborator Newton makes clear.
Cowper had, unlike Wesley or Watts or Newton, a twisted sensibility;
and if the twist gives to some of his hymns an incomparable power, some
of that power may be pathological.

It is idle to ask whether we could discern this, if we did not know the
special and painful circumstances in which Cowper's *Olney Hymns* were
composed. We do know those circumstances, as all but a few of his first
readers knew them. Cowper's terrible and tormented life was amply
documented almost as soon as he was dead. However, of those who sing

his hymns in church or chapel today, perhaps most do not know even the outline of this life; and their ignorance is what we must summon up as best we can, if Cowper's hymns are to be fairly considered as poems, rather than documents in 'a case'. The biographical facts are readily available; here they need not be rehearsed.

One of the Olney hymns that has been thought, if not pathological, certainly morbid, is 'Praise for the Fountain Opened':

> There is a fountain filled with blood
>   Drawn from Emmanuel's veins;
> And sinners, plunged beneath that flood,
>   Lose all their guilty stains.
>
> The dying thief rejoiced to see
>   That fountain in his day;
> And there have I, as vile as he,
>   Washed all my sins away.
>
> Dear dying Lamb, thy precious blood
>   Shall never lose its power,
> Till all the ransomed church of God
>   Be saved, to sin no more.
>
> E'er since, by faith, I saw the stream
>   Thy flowing wounds supply,
> Redeeming love has been my theme,
>   And shall be till I die.
>
> Then in a nobler, sweeter song,
>   I'll sing thy power to save;
> When this poor lisping, stammering tongue
>   Lies silent in the grave.
>
> Lord, I believe thou hast prepared
>   (Unworthy though I be)
> For me a blood-bought free reward,
>   A golden harp for me!
>
> 'Tis strung and tuned for endless years,
>   And formed by power divine,
> To sound in God the Father's ears
>   No other name but thine.

Vincent Newey[2] has boldly defended this as 'a fine hymn – in an idiom that is alien to us' – alien, that is, unless we are familiar with those 'stricter' dissenting chapels where, Newey assures us, such lines with

[2] Vincent Newey, *Cowper's Poetry. A Critical Study and Reassessment* (Liverpool, 1982), p. 296.

their blood-boltered imagery, 'still serve, when sung, as a valuable means of "rebinding" the congregation (or "Church") through a shared act of dedication to a highly separate order of experience; they have, in other words, the force of a liturgy'. In other words again, 'nobody steeped in the formulaic literalness of the Dissenting imagin-ation in its dealing with the Redeemer would be concerned with "meaning" in this context. Involvement in the "image" – the form of words and the mode of apprehension they embody – would be total.' This is to bear very hard on the perception that such a hymn is, and is meant to be, *congregational*; and certainly Newey is right to imply that it is no use approaching such poems expecting them to give us what we may have learned to value in for instance *The Temple* of George Herbert. All the same we may protest that morbidity is no less morbid when whole congregations share it; or, to put it another way, that the liturgical usefulness of a hymn cannot pre-empt our considering it in its character as a poem.

Rather plainly Cowper's 'fountain filled with blood' has something in common with Watts' 'His dying crimson, like a robe'. (And Watts was a Dissenter, as Cowper was not.) Vincent Newey certainly sees the connection, as when he points in Cowper's poem to 'baroque sensuous-ness'. But he sees too that Cowper's lines are near akin to Wesley's:

> Should any of thy Grace despair?
> To All, to All, Thy bowels move,
> But straitned in our own we are.

No baroque sensuousness there! And yet Newey's argument, invoking a nonconformist liturgy, would exonerate Wesley's lines as well as Cowper's. We may be sure that he is right about how such trains of imagery originate, and how Cowper, that genteel classicist, could be brought to utter them. But it is still possible to applaud Watts' lines even as we deplore Cowper's not much less than Wesley's.

However, this is not the characteristic idiom of the *Olney Hymns*. In many of them, and most of the best, the style is on the contrary exceptionally bare and unadorned, almost devoid of imagery:

> The Lord will happiness divine
> On contrite hearts bestow:
> Then tell me, gracious God, is mine
> A contrite heart or no?

> I hear, but seem to hear in vain,
> Insensible as steel:

If aught is felt, 'tis only pain
　　To find I cannot feel.

I sometimes think myself inclin'd
　　To love thee if I could;
But often feel another mind,
　　Averse to all that's good.

My best desires are faint and few,
　　I fain would strive for more;
But when I cry, 'My strength renew',
　　Seem weaker than before.

Thy saints are comforted, I know,
　　And love thy house of prayer;
I therefore go where others go,
　　But find no comfort there.

O make this heart rejoice or ache!
　　Decide this doubt for me;
And if it be not broken, break;
　　And heal it, if it be!

To Southey, still pursuing the critique of religious 'enthusiasm' that had sustained him also through his *Life of Wesley*, these sentiments seemed (though he does not use the word) morbid. But surely we must challenge him: these sentiments, which he would devalue by putting them in a case-history ('His malady in its latter stage had been what is termed religious madness'), are such as what even a tepid or torpid Christian might feel in all soberness, faced with the challenges that the Pauline epistles and *The Book of Common Prayer* throw down. Indeed Cowper's invaluable witness, speaking as he did from the pew not the pulpit, is precisely in articulating the feelings of the tepid or torpid communicant. This language is not 'liturgical'; it is on the contrary personal, and thereby representative.

The style is thoroughly, even scandalously, plain. And it is notable that Southey, when in the second volume of his *Life of Cowper* he offered a 'Sketch of English Poetry from Chaucer to Cowper', did not so much as notice 'the plain style'. This is hardly surprising, for it was only in the present century that this style was adequately isolated, described and illustrated by the poet-critic, Yvor Winters. It was Winters whom I eagerly and gratefully had in mind when those years ago I linked Cowper's name with Jonson's. For Ben Jonson is, in Winters' account of the matter, the prime example of the plain style in English. And I shall argue that what Winters claimed for Jonson can also be claimed for the best of Cowper's Olney hymns.

According to Winters,

the plain style eschews both impassioned oratory and the pomp of public ceremony. Its norm is a man speaking quietly to other men in the ordinary world. Its vision is not utopian. The poets of the plain style do not build the 'golden worlds' of which Sidney dreamed, but speak in the sober tones of those on whom (in Greville's phrase) the 'black ox' of experience has trod. Their poetry is a poetry of direct statement, the language almost wholly abstract, the organization generally logical, the themes broad, common, proverbial. It is a poetry ... saved from platitude only, and often narrowly, by the poet's skill in reanimating the emotional truth in the truism – in persuading the reader, through the precision of his statement and the rhythmical inflection of his voice, that he speaks not by rote but in the true accents of the experience whose authority he claims.[3]

If this is, as I find it, an admirably exact description of the sort of poetry we have in 'The Lord will happiness divine', it describes also other of the Olney hymns, which express sentiments less forlorn:

> No strength of Nature can suffice
>   To serve the Lord aright:
> And what she has she misapplies,
>   For want of clearer light.
>
> How long beneath the Law I lay
>   In bondage and distress;
> I toiled the precept to obey,
>   But toiled without success.
>
> Then to abstain from outward sin
>   Was more than I could do;
> Now, if I feel its power within,
>   I feel I hate it too.
>
> Then all my servile works were done
>   A righteousness to raise;
> Now, freely chosen in the Son,
>   I freely choose His ways.

---

[3] Terry Comito, *In Defense of Winters. The Poetry and Prose of Yvor Winters* (Madison, Wisconsin, 1986), pp. 154–5.

'What shall I do', was then the word
    'That I may worthier grow?'
'What shall I render to the Lord?'
    Is my inquiry now.

To see the law by Christ fulfilled,
    And hear His pardoning voice,
Changes a slave into a child,
    And duty into choice.

The point is really of some importance for the history of English poetry. For if Cowper did practise the plain style in some of his hymns (and in his several poems called 'Stanzas Subjoined to the Yearly Bill of Mortality of the Parish of All Saints, Northampton'), then he appears to be – according to current accounts of this admittedly specialized matter – the only poet thus to practise between the seventeenth century and the twentieth. (Winters, to be sure, did not find the plain style there – but only, we have reason to believe, because he did not think to look.) Vincent Newey may seem to give us all that we ask for when, discussing 'The Contrite Heart' ('The Lord will happiness divine') he takes note of the one and only simile in the poem ('Insensible as steel') and opines: 'For the rest, we have, in Coleridge's definition, "the neutral style, or that common to Prose and Poetry", a "uniform adherence to genuine, logical English".' Is this the answer – that in Coleridge's notion of 'the neutral style' we anticipate what Winters was to designate 'the plain style'? I think not. The relevant passage in Coleridge's *Biographia Literaria* has to do with the Elizabethan poet, Samuel Daniel:

This poet's well-merited epithet is that of the 'well-languaged Daniel'; but, likewise, and by the consent of his contemporaries, no less than of all succeeding critics, the 'prosaic Daniel'. Yet those who thus designate this wise and amiable writer ... willingly admit that there are to be found throughout his poems ... exquisite specimens of that style, which, as the neutral ground of prose and verse, is common to both.

The note of condescension is unmistakable. (And if Wordsworth in *The White Doe of Rylstone* schooled himself to Daniel, in doing so he flouted his mentor, Coleridge.) Not Jonson, nor any other of Winters' Elizabethan heroes of the plain style (Gascoigne, Ralegh, Fulke Greville) is noticed by Coleridge in this connection. Coleridge's 'neutral style' gives offence to no one – unless, possibly, to Wordsworth. Winters's 'plain style' is on the contrary militant, it is fighting talk. For him the plain style was not one style among many, but the one right and reliable style

– for him, for his pupils and for any one else who would attend.[4] Thus, to find the plain style in Cowper, rather than the 'neutral' style, is a matter of some moment.

Cowper mostly reserved *his* fighting talk for other issues than this. Yet if we impartially gather together his scattered comments on poetic style and diction, we find reason to think that he might have sympathized with Winters, if not in his acrimony, in his objectives and his motives.[5] Very interesting and characteristic is a letter of 1787, explaining how he came to write his stanzas for the annual 'bill of mortality' for a Northampton parish:

On Monday morning last, Sam brought me word that there was a man in the kitchen who desired to speak with me. I ordered him in. A plain, decent, elderly figure made its appearance, and being desired to sit, spoke as follows: 'Sir, I am clerk of the parish of All-saints in Northampton; brother of Mr. C. the upholsterer. It is customary for the person in my office to annex to a bill of mortality which he publishes at Christmas, a copy of verses. You will do me a great favour, Sir, if you would furnish me with one.' To this I replied, 'Mr. C. you have several men of genius in your town, why have you not applied to some of them? There is a namesake of yours in particular, C–, the statuary, who, everybody knows, is a first-rate maker of verses. He surely is the man of all the world for your purpose.' – 'Alas! Sir, I have heretofore borrowed help from him, but he is a gentleman of so much reading, that the people of our town cannot understand him.' I confess to you, my dear, I felt all the force of the compliment implied in this speech, and was almost ready to answer, perhaps, my good friend, they may find me unintelligible too for the same reason. But on asking him whether he had walked over to Weston on purpose to implore the assitance of my muse, and on his replying in the affirmative, I felt my mortified vanity a little consoled, and pitying the poor man's distress, which appeared to be considerable, promised to supply him. The wagon has accordingly gone this day to Northampton loaded in part with my effusions in the mortuary stile. A fig for poets who write epitaphs upon individuals! I have written *one*, that serves *two hundred* persons.

Cowper, when most hag-ridden by religious terrors, never lost his sense of the ludicrous. And in as much as he recognized this and deliberately

---

[4] Winters set down Daniel as 'a Petrarchist'. At the end of his life, when admittedly his judgement was clouded by justified resentment, Winters disposed of Daniel in four sentences; 'Of Samuel Daniel little need be said. His best poem is the sonnet beginning *Beauty, sweet love*; his best poems are all available in the standard anthologies and are well known. Like Sidney, he aims primarily at grace of expression; his tone is less exuberant than that of Sidney; his style is more consistently pure; he has less talent. His tone is one of polished melancholy' (*Forms of Discovery* (1967), p. 36).

[5] See Donald Davie, 'The Critical Principles of William Cowper', *The Cambridge Journal*, VII (1953), pp. 182–8.

cultivated comedy as a therapeutic device, this points to one undeniably heroic aspect of his character, though as author rather of 'The
Diverting History of John Gilpin' than of the *Olney Hymns*.

The comedy of this letter is not altogether to modern taste, since it
turns on Cowper's condescension (in the strict, not the opprobrious
sense); he and his correspondent are deliciously aware of the gulf in
social status between Cowper, securely of the gentry, and the respectable tradesman who calls on him. On the other hand, Cowper's
acknowledgement of the justice of the claim made on him, and his
complying with it, shows how much fellow-feeling and reciprocity
could still flourish in the provincial society of England in the 1780s,
unequal and hierarchical though it was. Cowper moreover took seriously the challenge to show himself more than 'a first-rate maker of
verses', and to write so that 'the people of our town' might understand
him. The proof is in the poems that he wrote to fulfil this contract; for
instance, the stanzas for Christmas 1792:

> Thankless for favours from on high,
>   Man thinks he fades too soon;
> Though 'tis his privilege to die,
>   Would he improve the boon.
>
> But he, not wise enough to scan
>   His best concerns aright,
> Would gladly stretch life's little span
>   To ages, if he might.
>
> To ages in a world of pain,
>   To ages, where he goes
> Galled by affliction's heavy chain,
>   And hopeless of repose.
>
> Strange fondness of the human heart,
>   Enamoured of its harm!
> Strange world, that costs it so much smart,
>   And still has power to charm.
>
> Whence has the world her magic power?
>   Why deem we Death a foe?
> Recoil from weary life's best hour,
>   And covet longer woe?
>
> The cause is Conscience; – Conscience oft
>   Her tale of guilt renews:
> Her voice is terrible, though soft,
>   And dread of Death ensues.

Then, anxious to be longer spared,
        Man mourns his fleeting breath:
And evils then seem light, compared
        With the approach of Death.

'Tis judgement shakes him; there's the fear
        That prompts the wish to stay:
He has incurred a long arrear,
        And must despair to pay.

Pay? – follow Christ, and all is paid:
        His death your peace ensures;
Think on the grave where *He* was laid,
        And calm descend to *yours*.

It was, we perceive, not just comedy that could save Cowper from the black dog that sat on his shoulders, the 'black ox' of adversity; at times what lifted the load was fellow-feeling with his obscure and anonymous neighbours.

This poem is not a hymn, though it could readily be adapted to that purpose, were there any church prepared to stomach the austerity of the consolation it offers. (It seems that there were such, in Northampton in 1792.) It is, however, thoroughly in the plain style, as we have had it expounded. Yvor Winters, who was a stoical unbeliever, would have resisted the poem. Yet it satisfies his criteria.

Not much of Cowper is like this. *The Task*, which brought him late but instant fame in his lifetime, is in a style at once more glittering and more emollient. And several of the hymns depend or turn upon images to a degree that the plain style frowns upon. This is true of some of the most famous and best-loved, such as 'God moves in a mysterious way'. This, however, is a special case since the circumstances of its composition were, if anecdote may be believed, peculiarly horrible – to the extent that, once we have been advised of this, we cannot suppress it from our awareness. Nor should we, surely. For once we have grasped that among the wonders that God in His mysterious way performs, there figures the suicidal insanity which intermittently He visits on his poet (and there is evidence that Cowper had this in mind), then the consolation that the hymn seems to offer is profoundly, and horribly, ambiguous. That ambiguity seems to come in and be allowed for, not exclusively indeed but mainly, through the images that the plain style, for this reason among others, abjures. Of this hymn accordingly we might want to say that, whereas its power is real and unforgettable, that power is pathological or (at least partly) 'sick'.

A clearer because less disturbing example of the problems that arise when the plain style is mixed with something else is the short hymn called (by Cowper, or else Newton) 'Jehovah our Righteousness':

> My God, how perfect are thy ways!
>   But mine polluted are;
> Sin twines itself about my praise,
>   And slides into my pray'r.
>
> When I would speak what thou hast done
>   To save me from my sin,
> I cannot make Thy mercies known
>   But self-applause creeps in.
>
> Divine desire, that holy flame
>   Thy grace creates in me,
> Alas! impatience is its name
>   When it returns to Thee.
>
> This heart, a fountain of vile thoughts,
>   How does it overflow,
> While self upon the surface floats
>   Still bubbling from below!
>
> Let others in the gaudy dress
>   Of fancied merit shine;
> The Lord shall be my righteousness;
>   The Lord for ever mine.

The second stanza is purely in the plain style. In the first, the image of sin as serpent is so muted and so conventional that it can be tolerated as 'plain'; as can be, in the third stanza, the 'holy flame'. But in the next stanza, 'Still bubbling from below!' cannot be thus accommodated; it creates in its context ambiguities that the final stanza can only make a show of resolving.

In Norman Nicholson's too seldom consulted *William Cowper* (1951), there is an extraordinary passage about Watts' use of scriptural allusions:

He drew largely from the Old Testament and he drew from it less as from a literature than as from a myth. Indeed, to Protestant England, and especially to Puritan England, the Old Testament had become the true national myth. To the theologians it may have been first and foremost the revelation of the pre-Christian God of the Jewish faith, but to the people it was also a great, rumbling, roaring balladry of heroes, prophets, battles, laments and victories. They accepted its historicity without question, of course, but they saw it also as a romance, where, through scenes as rich and festering as a tropical swamp, wandered the slayers with their slings and their thigh-bones, and the priests whose tongues crackled with fire. The bull died on the altar; the goat, with the sins of the people on its head, escaped to the wilderness; the living bird, dipped in the blood of the slain bird, flew off into the air. Thunderous names broke against the rock, cities grew on the bare limestone hills like bracken fungi on the trunk of a tree; armies moved their tents about the desert like brown rolling dunes. It was a landscape at once heroic and furtive. Animals came out of the darkness, lions, jackals and the little foxes, and in the warm, damp, secretive places grew a strange flora, almost unimaginable to English eyes: the Rose of Sharon, the Lily of the Valley, the vine, the palm and the gopher tree.

Here in this hot-house imagery, rare as the tiger-ridden jungles painted by the Douanier Rousseau, the hidden fancies of English Puritanism dreamed and explored. Milton drew on it magnificently; so also did Watts. To both of them, living in the hard tradition of seventeenth-century and early eighteenth-century Calvinism, the myth was a psychological necessity – it was the humus, the compost, the ferment and heat at the root, without which their imagination would never have budded and flowered. The early Methodists, on the other hand, because of the more exciting spiritual atmosphere in which they lived, needed the myth less: it was the historical truth of the Bible which mattered to them.

(Hence, Nicholson argues, the predominance of New Testament allusions in the poetry of Charles Wesley.) The inventive eloquence of such a passage establishes a reality that scholars must acknowledge, even as they confess that it could not have been arrived at by scholarly procedures, but only by poetic intuition.[6]

The absence from the *Olney Hymns* of this 'mythic' dimension (so thoroughly fleshed out in Nicholson's leaping prose) is what leads him to speak, roundly though regretfully, of 'Cowper's comparative failure as a hymn writer'. Such must indeed be the verdict, if one approaches these poems down an anthropological or socio-anthropological perspective (as Nicholson does, comparing at one point Wesley's hymns with that very 'anthropological' poem, Eliot's *The Waste Land*). Moreover one must concede that, beside poems like Eliot's (or Wesley's) which give one imaginative access to fertility-rituals, the *Olney Hymns* seem undeniably tame, thin-blooded – except for 'sports' like 'There is a fountain fill'd with blood', which Nicholson, like Newey after him,

---

[6] Scholars, however, would rightly jib at Milton's being called, without qualification, Calvinist.

predictably makes a sturdy claim for. The plain style, which defines itself by adjuring those more vivid effects that the non-plain styles seek out, will always, whether conveyed in pulpit eloquence or in poetry, attract fewer devotees.

And this is not the only way in which a reader or church-goer, fired by Watts' hymns, will think himself cheated when he gets to Cowper's. Watts has been called 'pompous'; he is certainly ceremonious. But the plain style, we remember, 'eschews both impassioned oratory and the pomp of public ceremony'. Eschewing is very much the way in which the plain style works; and the reader can respond properly only when he is aware of what is being eschewed, of the opportunities that the poet has passed up, not from incapacity but on principle. There is no wonder, and nothing shameful, if the common reader or church-goer finds himself incapable of such instructed fastidiousness.

Watts' ceremoniousness is often missed and as often misinterpreted. When in his most seemingly artless strain he starts out, 'We are a Garden wall'd around, / Chosen and made peculiar Ground', we are unprepared for, in the first place, a daring appropriation of the erotic idiom of the Song of Songs; and for, secondly, a quite defiant procla- mation of the dissenting subculture in the England of Queen Anne and George I.[7] With that declaration (missed, unless we reconstruct the historical circumstances), comes 'the pomp of public ceremony'. Cowper the Anglican, sixty years later, had no such consolidated 'we' to write out of, or to write for. In his most poignant hymns 'we' stands for the dispersed company of hesitant and demoralized worshippers like himself, believers indeed but continually conscious of falling short:

> To keep the lamp alive,
> With oil we fill the bowl;
> 'Tis water makes the willow thrive,
> And grace that feeds the soul.
>
> The Lord's unsparing hand
> Supplies the living stream;
> It is not at our own command,
> But still derived from him.
>
> Beware of Peter's word,
> Nor confidently say,
> 'I never will deny thee, Lord,' –
> But, – 'Grant I never may.'

---

[7] See Donald Davie, *A Gathered Church* (1978), pp. 28–32.

> Man's wisdom is to seek
>   His strength in God alone;
> And even an angel would be weak
>   Who trusted in his own.
>
> Retreat beneath his wings,
>   And in his grace confide!
> This more exalts the King of kings
>   Than all your works beside.
>
> In Jesus is our store,
>   Grace issues from his throne;
> Whoever says, 'I want no more',
>   Confesses he has none.

The concluding off-rhyme ('throne'/'none') – it has been anticipated in the second stanza – is a good example of how the plain style gets its effects by eschewing what other styles work hard for.

But as we might expect, Cowper is happier with 'I' than 'we':

> O Lord, my best desire fulfil,
>   And help me to resign
> Life, health, and comfort to thy will,
>   And make thy pleasure mine.
>
> Why should I shrink at thy command,
>   Whose love forbids my fears?
> Or tremble at the gracious hand
>   That wipes away my tears?
>
> No, rather let me freely yield
>   What most I prize to thee;
> Who never has a good withheld,
>   Or wilt withhold, from me.
>
> Thy favour, all my journey through,
>   Thou art engaged to grant;
> What else I want, or think I do,
>   'Tis better still to want.
>
> Wisdom and mercy guide my way,
>   Shall I resist them both?
> A poor blind creature of a day,
>   And crushed before the moth!
>
> But ah! my inward spirit cries,
>   Still bind me to thy sway;
> Else the next cloud that veils the skies
>   Drives all these thoughts away.

The man 'speaking quietly to other men in the ordinary world' could hardly be heard more clearly than in 'What else I want, or think I do'. And remarkably this holds for speakers in the twentieth century as for speakers in the eighteenth. This is what Cowper, like John Wesley before him, admired in Matthew Prior who had expostulated, 'Let us e'en talk a little like folks of this world.' Persistently as Cowper exhorts us to think of the next world, he never forgets, when he is writing verse, what belongs to *this* world. This is a charitably Anglican world, in so far as many of the people at worship are not sure why they are there, or whether they should be. Accordingly, though Cowper certainly looked back to Watts and looked up to him – 'a man', he said 'of true poetical ability ... frequently sublime in his conceptions and masterly in his executions' – he differed from him because he was differently situated in history. And part of the difference was that Cowper could write in the plain style whereas Watts could not, and, given his different circumstances, neither wanted nor needed to.

It was not the style of *Olney Hymns*, whether plain or un-plain (and some of the best are un-plain, for instance the lovely 'Sometimes a light surprises'), that earned a small fortune for Cowper's publishers after the poet's death. The hymns for instance were not in the mind of the insufferable matron who opined, as early as 1806, that 'The turgid attire of bombastic epithet, and the cold uninteresting accumulation of abstract ideas, so lately puffed into fashion, seems yielding to that force of feeling, elegant simplicity of expression, and lucid yet elevated arrangement of ideas, which characterized the happiest efforts of the muse in her days of exaltation.' The unthinking denigration of 'abstract ideas', parroted from that day to this, shows how hostile this is to the plain style, in which the language is 'almost wholly abstract'. And so it does Cowper no service at all when the writer goes on: 'The popularity of Cowper's poems has doubtless contributed to this happy change; in which the sterling grandeur of the thought, and the exquisite appropriateness of the imagery, compensate for carelessness of expression, or occasional untuneableness of the measure.'[8] This was the flaccid adulation of Cowper that provoked both Byron and Hazlitt into angry remonstrances. But their carping voices were heard only to be discounted; and fifty years later the biographers of James Montgomery could still speak of 'that improved style which the tender but unaffected

---

[8] Mrs West, *Letters to a Young Lady* (1806), vol. 2, pp. 457–8.

genius of Cowper had in a great measure suggested'.[9] It is impossible at this date to determine what these writers thought they meant by 'tender *but* unaffected'.

The purpose of this excursion into the history of Cowper's reputation is not to maintain, what would be absurd, that the author of *The Task* and 'The Castaway' went downhill from his first ventures in the *Olney Hymns*. It is to suggest that as a hymn-writer Cowper found an idiom which he could seldom or never use thereafter; and that his great popularity in the first half of the nineteenth century has thrown up a smoke-screen that we have to pierce in order to recognize this.

The Regency and the early years of Victoria were so partial to Cowper because plainly the Mrs Wests of those eras, along with minds more powerful and influential, saw him as groping towards what they or their contemporaries, they were sure, had achieved more securely. But this is a takeover bid that must be resisted. 'Secure' is a word that it is hard to use about Cowper; and yet there is an important sense in which he was, and felt that he was, secure. This is the lesson of the Letters: Cowper could most of the time function, despite his mental affliction, precisely because he could feel secure about for instance his rank in society. So long as he was allowed to shun the limelight, Cowper was thoroughly at home in the society of his time; at ease and self-possessed. The title of Lord David Cecils' long popular biography, *The Stricken Deer* (1929), has created a false impression. What Cowper writes of public affairs, for instance in his surprisingly robust political poems, tells a different story: he was not at odds with his society, nor out of key with his time. This has to be insisted on, because ever since the earliest Mrs Wests, up to the present day, Cowper has been denied the privilege of speaking for his own times, esteemed instead as harbinger and precursor of times that were to come. Yet Cowper was what he seems to be – an eighteenth-century poet, not an early 'Romantic'. And this is as true of his hymns as of his other poems.

It is interesting and important to remember in this connection that *Olney Hymns* was bitterly attacked, along with hymn-writing in general, by the prominent Evangelical, William Romaine. Cowper accordingly cannot be thought to speak for evangelicalism, as Wesley spoke for Methodism, or as Watts spoke for Independency or Old Dissent. In the 1770s there was not yet anything that could be called 'the Evangelical party' in the Church of England. On the contrary evangelicalism at

[9] John Holland and James Everett, *Memoirs of the Life and Writings of James Montgomery* (1855), vol. 2, pp. 1–2.

that time was a *movement*, a tide breaking down or washing over sectarian divisions. Newton thought of entering a nonconformist ministry; and some of his and Cowper's most cherished friends – for instance, the Reverend William Bull – were Dissenters. The temper of the times was indeed, among serious protestants, remarkably oecumenical – as it had not been fifty years before in the days of Watts and Swift, nor would be fifty years later, in the time of Robert Southey. Thus, when we say that Cowper had no consolidated 'we' to write out of or to write for, we should beware of construing this as a limitation. On the contrary, his writing for dispersed and anxious individuals (of whatever denomination or persuasion) is what gives his best hymns a distinctive urgency and pathos.

Moreover, when evangelicalism consolidated from a movement into a party, this was in line with a more general rigidifying and disuniting across the whole range of institutional protestantism through the first thirty years after Cowper's death. The causes of this are various, and some of them unclear. Sects proliferated: new ones like the Plymouth Brethren came into being; the Unitarians declared themselves, throwing off the wraps (most often Presbyterian) that they had sheltered under; and Methodism, after the deaths of the Wesley brothers, showed a notable proclivity for schism. Certainly by 1830 the fences between denominations, and between parties within denominations, had been re-erected and rose taller than ever. This sectarianism fostered, in congregations as well as from pulpits, in-group declamatory idioms beside which the plain style seemed insipid. Cowper's brief and sporadic recovery of that style is thus seen to be distinctly an eighteenth-century achievement.

Conclusion

Some fifty years ago Lord David Cecil, introducing his *Oxford Book of Christian Verse* (1940), decided that: 'Hymns are usually a second-rate type of poetry. Composed as they are for the practical purpose of congregational singing, they do not provide a free vehicle for the expression of the poet's imagination, his intimate soul. But for a rare exception like Campion, the Renaissance poets were at once too individual and too fanciful to write successful hymns. The Augustan manner of writing was far more appropriate to their production. And the bulk of our best hymns were [*sic*] written under its influence.' It is to be supposed that most people today still agree with Lord David; and none of the hymns that we have looked at have been put before the reader with any real hope that he will see them as more than masterpieces in (Cecil insists again later) 'their minor kind'.

Yet Cecil's distinction has to be taken on his sole authority. For we may agree that there are first-rate and second-rate poems, without conceding that there are first-rate and second-rate *types* of poetry, least of all when the distinction turns on the expression or non-expression of 'the poet's ... intimate soul'. For in one way the argument is obviously circular: we know whether the poet has been intimate with us only from what he has chosen to make public to us – his 'intimate soul' can be inferred only from what, since we encounter it in print, must be public utterance.

However, the clock is not to be put back. The Romantic Movement has happened; and Lord David Cecil writes in the after-surge of that Movement as certainly as John Keble, whose distinction between Primary Poets and Secondary Poets is rather plainly the rude ancestor of Cecil's distinction between first-rate and second-rate types of poetry. Moreover the Romantic Movement has irreversibly happened for many who have not read John Keble, nor busied themselves with literary history; most readers of poetry in the 1990s, however little they

155

know it and however eagerly the more knowing may subscribe themselves 'modernist' or 'post-modernist', proceed on Romantic presuppositions. And those presuppositions, as Cecil frankly admits, can only
obstruct the entrance to Watts' hymns or Smart's or John Newton's.

However, the name that can be avoided no longer is that of William
Blake (1757–1827). About Blake Cecil is admirably forthright: 'It is
doubtful whether he should appear in a book of Christian verse ... If he
was a Christian, he was certainly a heretic. His surprising gospel, with
its admiration for all positive feelings, its horror of any kind of pro-
hibition or asceticism, is at odds both with the doctrines of every
important branch of Christianity and also with Christ's own teaching.'
So much, we might think, for Blake as any sort of Christian poet. But
no! Lord David stifled his doubts without much trouble and represented Blake by eight poems. The anthologist excused himself by
pleading: 'But Blake, whether he would or no, was soaked through with
Christian thought: Christian symbols are an essential part of his native
language. And he was exquisitely responsive to certain phases of Christian sentiment ... Christian mercy, Christian humility, Christian compassion.' To the first of these pleas we may retort that 'Christian
symbols' are no more prominent in Blake than in other poets who do
not thereby earn the exclusive title, 'Christian'. Indeed this was
inevitable throughout the centuries when the Authorised Version of the
Scriptures was pre-eminently the book pressed upon English individuals in their impressionable years. Cecil's second plea must be taken
more seriously, since it seems to sanction as 'Christian' the practice of
endorsing certain Christian doctrines (those which inculcate mercy,
humility, compassion), while ignoring – or, as in Blake's case, explicitly
repudiating – other doctrines which are, or may seem to be, punitive
and exclusive. This practice was not common in Blake's lifetime nor for
many years after his death, for of course it was a long time before either
his poems or his pronouncements were taken seriously. By 1940,
however, the practice seems to have been widespread, and fifty years
later it sometimes seemed that the majority of professing Christians, not
just those many who avoided public worship, reserved to themselves the
right to ignore those of the Church's teachings as were not to their
liking. If so, David Cecil's inclusion of Blake may be thought to have
been vindicated: Blake's point of view, though unChristian in his
lifetime, has been accepted as Christian by later generations.

However, this line of thinking is surely hard to accept. Though many
people, including professing Christians, may think that Christian doc-

trine, like any other structure of human reason, is subject to the law of 'progress' – so that certain primitive doctrines may be thought to have been outworn – that cannot be so. Certain attitudes of the primitive Church – for instance, what seems to us its misogyny – may be, and doubtless ought to be, discredited. But this is quite different from thinking that its *doctrines* can be reconsidered and (some of them) discarded. The doctrines lock together in an intellectual structure; the failure or discrediting of one of its members weakens all the others, and threatens to overthrow the structure itself. Moreover, this is not altogether a structure of human reason, inasmuch as it rests on truths or axioms held to be *revealed*. In these undoubtedly contentious matters the faithful have lately looked in vain for guidance – certainly from the Church of England, which in the present century has consecrated more than one bishop who would not subscribe to either the virgin birth or the resurrection.

It is in this context that we can understand how William Blake, who wrote no hymns, has been endowed with one, posthumously:

> And did those feet in ancient time
> Walk upon England's mountains green?
> And was the holy Lamb of God
> On England's pleasant pastures seen?
>
> And did the Countenance Divine
> Shine forth upon our clouded hills?
> And was Jerusalem builded here
> Among these dark Satanic Mills?
>
> Bring me my Bow of burning gold!
> Bring me my Arrows of desire!
> Bring me my Spear! O clouds, unfold!
> Bring me my Chariot of fire!
>
> I will not cease from Mental Fight,
> Nor shall my Sword sleep in my hand,
> Till we have built Jerusalem
> In England's green and pleasant land.[1]

These verses were originally part of a Preface to Blake's *Milton*, a long poem in two books, written and etched 1804–8. The rest of the Preface consists of two paragraphs in prose which are interesting because they show that Blake's conscious intention in the verses was much more

[1] See for instance *The BBC Hymnbook* (1951).

narrowly polemical than we might suppose. (The polemic is not overtly political, any more than it is religious.) But ultimately this is beside the point, for it is not in the minds of those who heartily sing the verses – for instance, in football stadiums – at the present day. Those singers undoubtedly think that what they are singing is a hymn. By extricating the verses from the intricate context that Blake devised for them, we have made of them a poem that floats free, so free indeed as to mean all things to virtually all men (and women). It is to be hoped for instance that others besides out-and-out pacifists will thrill to the notion of 'Mental Fight'. If this endows the pacifist with the martial imagery of bow and arrows and spear, chariot and sword, at the same time as it exempts him from shedding blood or even breaking heads, this is a thoroughly legitimate and imaginative translation of much in the Book of Psalms. And at the same time the pacifist can quite honourably join in a sentiment of exalted patriotism.

What exalts the sentiment is partly the substitution of mental for physical combat. But more pervasively what exalts is the interweaving of the patriotic theme with scriptural images like 'Jerusalem' and 'holy Lamb'.[2] And it is here we run into difficulty. For on what grounds are the patriotic and the scriptural themes interwoven? The grounds are at best mythological, certainly they are unargued. Indeed, if we look, the poem has no *argument* at all. And whereas this did not matter in the place that Blake devised for these verses, it matters greatly and (we may think) grievously when they are made to stand on their own as supposedly a self-sufficient poem or hymn. At all events, the lack of an argument differentiates this piece from all those we have considered in previous pages, as does of course Blake's presuming that he could pick and choose among doctrines. Not many later hymns are so innocent of argument as this one that we call 'Jerusalem'. But Blake all the same was a portent. And that is why this book must end with him, or (more precisely) some time before he took the stage.

---

[2] It has been pointed out that the 'dark Satanic Mills' are also scriptural, in so far as they allude to the labours of Samson, 'Eyeless in Gaza at the mill with slaves'.

Index

CAMBRIDGE STUDIES IN EIGHTEENTH-CENTURY
ENGLISH LITERATURE AND THOUGHT